4575-94

ENVIRONMENTAL ACTION GROUPS

EARTH • AT • RISK

ENVIRONMENTAL ACTION GROUPS

by Robbin Lee Zeff

Introduction by
Russell E. Train

Chairman of the Board
of Directors,
World Wildlife Fund and
The Conservation Foundation

CHELSEA HOUSE PUBLISHERS

new york   philadelphia

CHELSEA HOUSE PUBLISHERS

EDITORIAL DIRECTOR: Richard Rennert
EXECUTIVE MANAGING EDITOR: Karyn Gullen Browne
EXECUTIVE EDITOR: Sean Dolan
COPY CHIEF: Robin James
PICTURE EDITOR: Adrian G. Allen
ART DIRECTOR: Robert Mitchell
MANUFACTURING DIRECTOR: Gerald Levine
PRODUCTION COORDINATOR: Marie Claire Cebrián-Ume

EARTH AT RISK
SENIOR EDITOR: Jake Goldberg

Staff for *Environmental Action Groups*
EDITORIAL ASSISTANTS: Robert Green, Mary B. Sisson
SENIOR DESIGNER: Marjorie Zaum
PICTURE RESEARCHER: Villette Harris
COVER ILLUSTRATION: Bryce Lee

This book is printed on recycled paper.

First Printing

1 3 5 7 9 8 6 4 2

Library of Congress Cataloging-in-Publication Data
Zeff, Robbin Lee.
  Environmental action groups/Robbin Lee Zeff; introductory
essay by Russell E. Train.
  p. cm.—(Earth at risk)
  Includes bibliographical references and index.
  Summary: Discusses the history of environmentalism in the
United States, including background on such groups as the Sierra
Club, Greenpeace, the Nature Conservancy, Environmental
Action, and a variety of anti-nuclear organizations.
  ISBN 0-7910-1593-9
        0-7910-1618-8 (pbk.)
  1. Green movement—United States—History—Juvenile
literature. [1. Green movement—History. 2. Environmental
protection—History. 3. Nature conservation—History.] I. Title.
II. Series.   93-836
GE197.Z44 1993   CIP
363.7'0525'0973—dc20   AC

CONTENTS

INTRODUCTION

Russell E. Train

Administrator, Environmental Protection Agency, 1973 to 1977; Chairman of the Board of Directors, World Wildlife Fund and The Conservation Foundation

There is a growing realization that human activities increasingly are threatening the health of the natural systems that make life possible on this planet. Humankind has the power to alter nature fundamentally, perhaps irreversibly.

This stark reality was dramatized in January 1989 when *Time* magazine named Earth the "Planet of the Year." In the same year, the Exxon *Valdez* disaster sparked public concern over the effects of human activity on vulnerable ecosystems when a thick blanket of crude oil coated the shores and wildlife of Prince William Sound in Alaska. And, no doubt, the 20th anniversary celebration of Earth Day in April 1990 renewed broad public interest in environmental issues still further. It is no accident then that many people are calling the years between 1990 and 2000 the "Decade of the Environment."

And this is not merely a case of media hype, for the 1990s will truly be a time when the people of the planet Earth learn the meaning of the phrase "everything is connected to everything else" in the natural and man-made systems that sustain our lives. This will be a period when more people will understand that burning a tree in Amazonia adversely affects the global atmosphere just as much as the exhaust from the cars that fill our streets and expressways.

Central to our understanding of environmental issues is the need to recognize the complexity of the problems we face and the relationships between environmental and other needs in our society. Global warming provides an instructive example. Controlling emissions of carbon dioxide, the principal greenhouse gas, will involve efforts to reduce the use of fossil fuels to generate electricity. Such a reduction will include energy conservation and the promotion of alternative energy sources, such as nuclear and solar power.

The automobile contributes significantly to the problem. We have the choice of switching to more energy-efficient autos and, in the longer run, of choosing alternative automotive power systems and relying more on mass transit. This will require different patterns of land use and development, patterns that are less transportation and energy intensive.

In agriculture, rice paddies and cattle are major sources of greenhouse gases. Recent experiments suggest that universally used nitrogen fertilizers may inhibit the ability of natural soil organisms to take up methane, thus contributing tremendously to the atmospheric loading of that gas—one of the major culprits in the global warming scenario.

As one explores the various parameters of today's pressing environmental challenges, it is possible to identify some areas where we have made some progress. We have taken important steps to control gross pollution over the past two decades. What I find particularly encouraging is the growing environmental consciousness and activism by today's youth. In many communities across the country, young people are working together to take their environmental awareness out of the classroom and apply it to everyday problems. Successful recycling and tree-planting projects have been launched as a result of these budding environmentalists who have committed themselves to a cleaner environment. Citizen action, activated by youthful enthusiasm, was largely responsible for the fast-food industry's switch from rainforest to domestic beef, for pledges from important companies in the tuna industry to use fishing techniques that would not harm dolphins, and for the recent announcement by the McDonald's Corporation to phase out polystyrene "clam shell" hamburger containers.

Despite these successes, much remains to be done if we are to make ours a truly healthy environment. Even a short list of persistent issues includes problems such as acid rain, ground-level ozone and smog, and airborne toxins; groundwater protection and nonpoint sources of pollution, such as runoff from farms and city streets; wetlands protection; hazardous waste dumps; and solid waste disposal, waste minimization, and recycling.

Similarly, there is an unfinished agenda in the natural resources area: effective implementation of newly adopted management plans for national forests; strengthening the wildlife refuge system; national park management, including addressing the growing pressure of development on lands surrounding the parks; implementation of the Endangered Species Act; wildlife trade problems, such as that involving elephant ivory; and ensuring adequate sustained funding for these efforts at all levels of government. All of these issues are before us today; most will continue in one form or another through the year 2000.

Each of these challenges to environmental quality and our health requires a response that recognizes the complex nature of the problem. Narrowly conceived solutions will not achieve lasting results. Often it seems that when we grab hold of one part of the environmental balloon, an unsightly and threatening bulge appears somewhere else.

The higher environmental issues arise on the national agenda, the more important it is that we are armed with the best possible knowledge of the economic costs of undertaking particular environmental programs and the costs associated with not undertaking them. Our society is not blessed with unlimited resources, and tough choices are going to have to be made. These should be informed choices.

All too often, environmental objectives are seen as at cross-purposes with other considerations vital to our society. Thus, environmental protection is often viewed as being in conflict with economic growth, with energy needs, with agricultural productions, and so on. The time has come when environmental considerations must be fully integrated into every nation's priorities.

One area that merits full legislative attention is energy efficiency. The United States is one of the least energy efficient of all the industrialized nations. Japan, for example, uses far less energy per unit of gross national product than the United States does. Of course, a country as large as the United States requires large amounts of energy for transportation. However, there is still a substantial amount of excess energy used, and this excess constitutes waste. More fuel-efficient autos and home heating systems would save millions of barrels of oil, or their equivalent, each year. And air pollutants, including greenhouse gases, could be significantly reduced by increased efficiency in industry.

I suspect that the environmental problem that comes closest to home for most of us is the problem of what to do with trash. All over the world, communities are wrestling with the problem of waste disposal. Landfill sites are rapidly filling to capacity. No one wants a trash and garbage dump near home. As William Ruckelshaus, former EPA administrator and now in the waste management business, puts it, "Everyone wants you to pick up the garbage and no one wants you to put it down!"

At the present time, solid waste programs emphasize the regulation of disposal, setting standards for landfills, and so forth. In the decade ahead, we must shift our emphasis from regulating waste disposal to an overall reduction in its volume. We must look at the entire waste stream, including product design and packaging. We must avoid creating waste in the first place. To the greatest extent possible, we should then recycle any waste that is produced. I believe that, while most of us enjoy our comfortable way of life and have no desire to change things, we also know in our hearts that our "disposable society" has allowed us to become pretty soft.

Land use is another domestic issue that might well attract legislative attention by the year 2000. All across the United States, communities are grappling with the problem of growth. All too often, growth imposes high costs on the environment—the pollution of aquifers; the destruction of wetlands; the crowding of shorelines; the loss of wildlife habitat; and the loss of those special places, such as a historic structure or area, that give a community a sense of identity. It is worth noting that growth is not only the product of economic development but of population movement. By the year 2010, for example, experts predict that 75% of all Americans will live within 50 miles of a coast.

It is important to keep in mind that we are all made vulnerable by environmental problems that cross international borders. Of course, the most critical global conservation problems are the destruction of tropical forests and the consequent loss of their biological capital. Some scientists have calculated extinction rates as high as 11 species per hour. All agree that the loss of species has never been greater than at the present time; not even the disappearance of the dinosaurs can compare to today's rate of extinction.

In addition to species extinctions, the loss of tropical forests may represent as much as 20% of the total carbon dioxide loadings to the atmosphere. Clearly, any international approach to the problem of global warming must include major efforts to stop the destruction of forests and to manage those that remain on a renewable basis. Debt for nature swaps, which the World Wildlife Fund has pioneered in Costa Rica, Ecuador, Madagascar, and the Philippines, provide a useful mechanism for promoting such conservation objectives.

Global environmental issues inevitably will become the principal focus in international relations. But the single overriding issue facing the world community today is how to achieve a sustainable balance between growing human populations and the earth's natural systems. If you travel as frequently as I do in the developing countries of Latin America, Africa, and Asia, it is hard to escape the reality that expanding human populations are seriously weakening the earth's resource base. Rampant deforestation, eroding soils, spreading deserts, loss of biological diversity, the destruction of fisheries, and polluted and degraded urban environments threaten to spread environmental impoverishment, particularly in the tropics, where human population growth is greatest.

It is important to recognize that environmental degradation and human poverty are closely linked. Impoverished people desperate for land on which to grow crops or graze cattle are destroying forests and overgrazing even more marginal land. These people become trapped in a vicious downward spiral. They have little choice but to continue to overexploit the weakened resources available to them. Continued abuse of these lands only diminishes their productivity. Throughout the developing world, alarming amounts of land rendered useless by over-grazing and poor agricultural practices have become virtual wastelands, yet human numbers continue to multiply in these areas.

From Bangladesh to Haiti, we are confronted with an increasing number of ecological basket cases. In the Philippines, a traditional focus of U.S. interest, environmental devastation is widespread as deforestation, soil erosion, and the destruction of coral reefs and fisheries combine with the highest population growth rate in Southeast Asia.

Controlling human population growth is the key factor in the environmental equation. World population is expected to at least double to about 11 billion before leveling off. Most of this growth will occur in the poorest nations of the developing world. I would hope that the United States will once again become a strong advocate of international efforts to promote family planning. Bringing human populations into a sustainable balance with their natural resource base must be a vital objective of U.S. foreign policy.

Foreign economic assistance, the program of the Agency for International Development (AID), can become a potentially powerful tool for arresting environmental deterioration in developing countries. People who profess to care about global environmental problems— the loss of biological diversity, the destruction of tropical forests, the greenhouse effect, the impoverishment of the marine environment, and so on—should be strong supporters of foreign aid planning and the principles of sustainable development urged by the World Commission on Environment and Development, the "Brundtland Commission."

If sustainability is to be the underlying element of overseas assistance programs, so too must it be a guiding principle in people's practices at home. Too often we think of sustainable development only in terms of the resources of other countries. We have much that we can and should be doing to promote long-term sustainability in our own resource management. The conflict over our own rainforests, the old growth forests of the Pacific Northwest, illustrates this point.

The decade ahead will be a time of great activity on the environmental front, both globally and domestically. I sincerely believe we will be tested as we have been only in times of war and during the Great Depression. We must set goals for the year 2000 that will challenge both the American people and the world community.

Despite the complexities ahead, I remain an optimist. I am confident that if we collectively commit ourselves to a clean, healthy environment we can surpass the achievements of the 1980s and meet the serious challenges that face us in the coming decades. I hope that today's students will recognize their significant role in and responsibility for bringing about change and will rise to the occasion to improve the quality of our global environment.

John Muir (right), founder of the Sierra Club, is pictured here with Theodore Roosevelt. During his administration, Roosevelt doubled the number of national parks and created the first 50 national wildlife refuges.

chapter 1

A CENTURY
OF CONCERN

In 1988 a team of environmentalists from the international organization Greenpeace took a tour down the
Mississippi River to investigate the sources and consequences
of its contamination. The team questioned people who lived
along the Mississippi, asking what they thought about the
pollution, how it personally affected them, and what they were
doing about it. Examining the effects on local residents of the
chemical contamination of the mighty Mississippi infused the
facts with emotion and controversy.

Environmentalists found that factories poured tons of
toxic waste into the Mississippi River every day. Brown mucky
blotches foamed near the shores of the levee, and thick swirls of
fluorescent colors floated sluggishly on the surface. From the
mouth of the Great Lakes to the Gulf of Mexico, the Mississippi
River was choking to death.

Local people told the inquisitive visitors about life along
the Mississippi. A mother stroked the bald head of her young
daughter while recounting the child's battle with leukemia,
allegedly caused by carcinogenic pollutants dumped into the

Mississippi. A man discussed how his fellow factory workers got sick from the chemicals they handled. And a retired military officer told the environmentalists how enraged he was that our great nation could let things get so out of hand.

Surprisingly, the tour ended on a note of hope. All along the river people were doing something about the pollution. Moms and dads, farmers and factory workers, and students and teachers were organizing environmental action groups. One woman, with a voice coarse and scratchy from a respiratory disease, explained how her community formed an organization to fight a local industrial plant whose incinerator puffed black smoke into the air. The group's interest in the incinerator revealed other local problems; the local landfill was leaking into their water supply, and a nearby wilderness area was threatened by highway expansion. The same group that formed around a single problem—the incinerator—was now working to find solutions to many of its community's environmental problems.

Not every community forms a new environmental group. Some use the local chapters of existing organizations, such as the Sierra Club, the Audubon Society, or the Izaak Walton League, to deal with local issues. Whether joining groups born out of local communities or chapters of larger organizations, people along the Mississippi are amassing an army of concerned citizens to clean up the river.

What are the objectives of environmental groups, and how do they operate? All groups try to educate the public on their specific concerns. Some local groups go door-to-door to inform their neighbors that factories are dumping waste directly into local water sources or how the community can make recycling work in their town. Other groups lobby politicians or speak at city council meetings, churches, or public hearings. And sometimes groups express their concerns through rallies, protests, and parades. Industry and lenient environmental laws are responsible for the pollution of the Mississippi River, but people in local and national groups are joining forces to make life along the river clean and safe once again.

The history of the pollution of the Mississippi River is more than just the history of derelict industrial practices. Environmental crises are often presented as a collection of disconnected factors. But in the stories of the people that live along the Mississippi's banks, the human consequences of environmental contamination unfold. When the consequences of pollution were limited or even speculative, few citizens felt the need to get involved. Today pollution touches nearly everyone; from the hovering, gray, smog-filled skies over Los Angeles to the Hazard: No Swimming signs on rivers and lakes across the nation, environmental problems are in everyone's backyard.

Thousands of environmental action groups exist today, addressing water contamination, wilderness conservation, wildlife

Early conservationists sought to preserve the pristine beauty of the wilderness and to protect the natural habitats of game animals from the destruction caused by loggers and industrialists.

protection, and many other issues. The first environmental groups formed to protect wilderness areas and their inhabitants. Over the years, however, other concerns have surfaced, such as air and water pollution, global warming, and the need for clean, reliable energy sources. Each time a crisis has arisen, people have organized groups to defend the environment.

Environmental action groups embody an American tradition of civic virtue and the formation of civic associations. "Nothing, in my opinion, is more deserving of our attention than the intellectual and moral associations of America," wrote Alexis de Tocqueville, a French nobleman who traveled throughout the United States in the early 1800s and authored a classic treatise on the American way of life, *Democracy in America,* in 1835. "As soon as several of the inhabitants of the United States have taken up an opinion or a feeling which they wish to promote in the world, they look out for mutual assistance. And as soon as they have found each other out, they combine. From that moment they are no longer isolated men, but a power seen from afar, whose actions serve for an example, and whose language is listened to." During Tocqueville's time, the nation was young and wilderness conservation only a nascent concept, but when the need for preservation developed in the last decade of the 1800s, groups would form, just as Tocqueville had predicted.

"Why form a group?" asks an environmental leader, "One single person can yell all day. But when you've got a group, people listen." Environmental action groups demonstrate to the public that a collection of people share the same view and are willing to work toward a common goal. Groups publicize environmental problems by informing the public and drawing media coverage.

Why did people band together specifically around the issues of conservation and preservation? When did the wilderness become threatened? And what prompted this concern for nature? The story begins with the early American colonists.

THE WILDERNESS EXPERIENCE

The wilderness was one of the most important resources of the New World. The early European explorers crossed the Atlantic Ocean in search of India and its fabled treasures. Instead of finding the riches of India, they found a new land teeming with resources scarce in Europe. The forests sprouted pine, oak, and maple trees that could be used for the construction of ships and houses. The same forests offered antelope, deer, and other wild game to the hunter, and the fields provided rich, fertile soil for the farmer. The original colonists embarked on their journey across the ocean seeking political and religious freedom and adventure, but the vast physical wealth of America lured hordes more. To the men and women of the early colonies, the new land's bounties were endless.

The early explorers and colonists found the New World vastly different from the civilization they left in Europe; a dangerous and uncivilized wilderness that they saw as an obstacle between themselves and their paradise. As the Bible says, "Be fruitful, and multiply, and replenish the earth and subdue it, and have dominion over the fish of the sea and over the birds of the air and over every living thing that moveth upon the earth" (Gen. 1:28). Clearing and domesticating the wilderness became one of the highest priorities of colonial life. Natural resources were classified as a usable and expendable commodity.

Building a nation in the New World would entail taming the wilderness.

The Indians' attitude about land use differed from that of the colonists. The Indians took only what they needed from the land. The colonists, on the other hand, believed they could improve the land's productivity through ownership and cultivation. The European settlers became the primary agents of environmental change in the new world.

By the mid-18th century America was struggling to establish a sovereign identity. America lacked the architectural history of Europe, with its grand castles, towers, and cathedrals. But the young nation turned to her natural treasures—the land and its resources—for symbols of identity and greatness. America's rugged mountains, fertile valleys, and abundant streams became the pride of the American people. And yet these natural resources remained usable and expendable, to be consumed in America's race to become civilized.

Early rumblings in the Plymouth Colony in the 1620s and 1630s about managing the forests were motivated by resource availability and allocation rather than protection. An interest in permanently protecting and preserving the environment arose only when America reached a pivotal point in its development as a nation. The nation was becoming more urbanized, with densely populated cities and factory-lined rivers. Open land for sportsmen and naturalists alike dwindled, yielding to the demands of settlements and development.

In 1896, Frederick Jackson Turner argued in the magazine *Atlantic* that the American qualities of individualism and independence, and even America's system of democracy, developed out of the wilderness experience. Turner knew that the America of unlimited space was being fenced in. In 1890 the U.S. Census had reported that there was no longer a physical line separating civilization and wilderness. Settlers spanned the continent from coast to coast. With the closing of the frontier came the realization that the wilderness was a conquerable, and even fragile, resource, even as it symbolized the rugged American experience.

From the early colonial days to the mid-1880s, a few Americans espoused the need to protect the virtues of nature. But not until a wider constituency voiced its interest in preserving the wilderness did the problem garner national attention. A wilderness that needed to be tamed and conquered became one that needed to be conserved and defended. Over the past century what had begun as concern for wilderness and wildlife has expanded, by necessity, to the preservation of the very air we breathe and the water we drink.

ENVIRONMENTAL ACTION GROUPS

"Why did we start our group?" replied Sue Greer of People Against Hazardous Landfill Sites (PAHLS) in Valparaiso, Indiana. "It's a classic story really. The same reason why a lot of groups form today. We started our group in 1981 to fight the Wheeler landfill. We didn't want a landfill in our small town. Who would?" The PAHLS story is a common tale of citizens working together to stop a landfill or other waste-disposal facility from being put in their backyard.

Grass-roots organizations like PAHLS represent the newest link in a long chain of environmental action groups. Over the past hundred years, thousands of these groups have formed. In

Young demonstrators protest in front of the European Commission Headquarters in Brussels, sending a grave message about the possible effects of acid rain.

the early 1900s groups formed to conserve the wilderness; later, in the 1960s and 1970s, groups worked to protect many facets of the environment.

The development of environmental groups mirrors the long history of America's relationship with the environment. Americans have moved from fearing the wilderness to exploiting the wilderness to protecting the air, water, and land.

The development of environmental action groups can be divided into three periods. The first spans 60 years, from the closing of the American frontier to the 1950s, and is concerned chiefly with wilderness conservation. The second started with the social and political movements of the 1960s. In the third, a populist movement, beginning with grass-roots organizations and capturing the attention of governments around the world, has grown from seeds planted in the activism of the 1960s.

The early period, beginning in the 1890s, brought us such groups as the Sierra Club (1892), the Audubon Society (1905), the Wilderness Society (1935), the National Wildlife Federation (1936), Defenders of Wildlife (1947), the Conservation Foundation (1948), and many others. Naturalists, sportsmen, and professionals—the members of these groups—sought to conserve rich open spaces for wildlife refuges and recreational purposes. In this early period, conservation was primarily an intellectual debate, argued by an educated minority, that centered around wilderness and wildlife protection. The people active during the conservation period divided themselves into two camps. On the one side were naturalists who recognized a moral responsibility to protect wilderness in its virgin splendor. On the other were land managers who advocated the science of forest management.

The second period of environmental interest arose with the activism of the 1960s and 1970s. Alongside the Vietnam War and civil rights, the environment became a pressing issue. During this time, scientists, lawyers, and scholars started to examine their ethical and moral debt for the consequences of modern technology and formed groups like the World Wildlife Fund (1961), the Environmental Defense Fund (1967), and the Natural Resources Defense Council (1970).

At the same time, college students were rebelling against traditional conservative values and demanding political and corporate accountability. Many followed Ralph Nader in the formation of public interest research groups (PIRGs) on college campuses, such as CALPIRG in California or INPIRG in Indiana. Students demonstrated against the wasteful practices of government and industry and linked environmental destruction to America's wasteful habits.

Whereas the early conservationists focused primarily on preserving the wilderness in its pristine beauty, 50 years later environmentalists indicated that not only were wilderness areas threatened; the quality of air and water were in danger as well. They argued that humans would be the next endangered species if they failed to alter their course. Some organizations from the early conservation period became more aggressive during the 1960s, such as the Sierra Club, while new organizations, like Environmental Action (1970), captured the energy and enthusiasm of youthful leadership.

By the end of the 1970s, environmental activism became a local phenomenon. Communities discovered landfills that leaked chemicals into their groundwater and factories that discarded wastewater into rivers and streams. Neighborhood

Four Greenpeace ecoteurs unfurl a banner on the scaffolding that encases the Statue of Liberty to protest underground nuclear testing.

associations formed to address local situations. These groups did not want the waste discarded in their backyard or in anyone else's. They linked health problems to chemical contamination. Local communities began to look at waste-disposal practices as an issue of social justice; they were being dumped on because they lived in low-income and minority communities; a practice that led to the coining of the term "environmental justice." The new type of local activism that resulted differed from its predecessors by its broad grass-roots membership base. National organizations that formed out of grass-roots involvement include the Citizens' Clearinghouse for Hazardous Waste (1981) and the National Toxics Campaign (1985), as well as thousands of local groups across the country. As the environment became more of a local issue, fought in city and county council meetings and through local elections, women—mostly mothers—took leadership positions.

With the dawn of the 1990s, heralded as the decade of the environment, environmentalism expanded globally. A number of threats—among them the greenhouse effect, ocean dumping, and the destruction of tropical rain forests—brought environmental action groups from different nations together.

Environmental action groups continue to grow in number and in scope of interest. They provide an exciting opportunity to learn about changes in the land from a people-oriented perspective. Who are these environmental action groups? Why are there so many groups? What are the differences and similarities between the organizations? And how are these organizations making a difference in cleaning up the environment? With these questions the chronicle of environmental action begins.

Gifford Pinchot rests from his campaign for the Republican gubernatorial seat in Pennsylvania. Pinchot was chief of the U.S. Forest Service from 1898 to 1910 and founder of the National Conservation Association.

C O N S E R V I N G
A M E R I C A ' S   W I L D E R N E S S

In less than a century America was transformed from a wild, savage, and untamed land to a sprawling, domesticated giant. The pioneers' pride in taming the land is reflected in an entry from a settler's guidebook: "You look around and whisper, 'I vanquished this wilderness and made the chaos pregnant with order and civilization, alone I did it.'" The young nation looked on the settlement of the West as one of its greatest accomplishments.

The rapid destruction of vast expanses of wildland in the name of building a nation prompted the birth of conservation in the mid-1800s. The term *conservation* was coined by Gifford Pinchot and a fellow Forest Service official to denote the relationship between preservation and management of resources.

The Frenchman Alexis de Tocqueville, who traveled in America in 1831, believed that people who lived in urban areas place the highest value on nature. Tocqueville traced his own attraction to the wilderness to the fact that his roots were in a highly developed region of Europe. Within 50 years of the nation's founding, many Americans lived in urban areas far from the open frontier. The closing of the American frontier at the turn of the century brought many into the same urban circumstances that inspired Tocqueville's wilderness worship.

Moreover, the surge of westward expansion coupled with industrialization consumed the very resources that provided the nation with strength and identity. In the American wilderness lay the foundation for many of the nation's most cherished national characteristics: virility, ruggedness, and determination.

In crowded cities, the wilderness began to assume a different, almost mythological, presence in people's imaginations. Untouched forests and open land were seen as places of virtue and goodness to the grandchildren of the settlers who had aggressively sought to subdue the untamed land. Images of chaos and disorder that once described the wilderness became synonymous with urban life. Upton Sinclair's novel *The Jungle* presented Chicago's stockyards as a symbol of the satanic horrors of the "urban jungle." A new generation of Americans believed that the dangers of civilization, not of the wilderness, marked the root of the nation's troubles. Soon the people voiced their opinion, and the slow wheels of government began to turn.

The setting aside of the Arkansas Hot Springs as a natural reservation in 1832 was one of the first instances of government involvement in wilderness preservation. Next came a federal grant to California, making Yosemite Valley a federally protected park in 1864. Then, on March 1, 1872, President Ulysses S. Grant launched the federal government's official involvement in forest and wildlife conservation by designating over 2 million acres of northwestern Wyoming as the first national park, named Yellowstone. This historic act marked the beginning of large-scale federal wilderness preservation.

The earliest conservation groups formed at this time. Hunters, desirous to protect the habitat of their prey, were the first organized conservationists. Beginning in 1844, the New York Sportsmen's Club lobbied for stricter laws to protect game for hunting. The Boone and Crockett Club, a similar organization, was cofounded by Teddy Roosevelt and George Bird Grinnell, editor of *Forest and Stream*, some forty years later. The goal of the Boone and Crockett Club was to preserve land for big-game hunting. To become a member, a candidate had to prove that he had killed at least three big-game animals. Though the heads of slaughtered beasts adorned members' homes and clubs, their work preserved wild areas for big game to roam.

The El Capitan monolith in Yosemite, California. Yosemite became a national park in 1890.

Early conservationists were often wealthy gentlemen, scholars, sportsman, and naturalists who volunteered time, effort, and money to develop organizations to bring the plight of the vanishing wilderness to the attention of the nation.

The early conservationists were motivated by the desire to protect the trees in the forests, the fish in the streams, and the birds in the sky. Three conservation groups, the Sierra Club, the Audubon Society, and the Izaak Walton League, illustrate the attitudes and practices of organizations from this early period of conservation.

THE SIERRA CLUB

One of the oldest environmental groups still active today is the Sierra Club. The early history of the club chronicles the actions of John Muir, its founder and first president. Born in Scotland in 1838 and raised on a Wisconsin farm, Muir attended the University of Wisconsin, where he studied natural science and philosophy, but left the university to pursue other interests before taking a degree. He was good with his hands and invented mechanical equipment. A work-related accident at a carriage factory in Indianapolis nearly blinded him; and the convalescing Muir went on a thousand-mile walk through Kentucky, Tennessee, Georgia, and Florida to seek spiritual refuge in the wilderness. His travels took him to the Gulf of Mexico, where he set sail for California. Upon arrival in San Francisco in 1868, the story is told, he asked the first person he met the way out of town. The stranger pointed east, and Muir followed that path, which led him through the San Joaquin Valley to a place in the Sierra Nevadas known as Yosemite.

In Yosemite, Muir found the spiritual comfort he sought from his pristine surroundings and from the writings of Ralph Waldo Emerson, which he had brought with him to the high country. Emerson was a leader of the transcendentalist movement, which looked at nature as part of the soul of man and intimately tied to the web of life. For the transcendentalists, God and man were connected through nature.

The designation of Yosemite as a national park in 1890 inspired a group of northern Californian outdoorsmen to discuss the formation of an alpine club. Two years later, 27 prominent professors, scientists, politicians, and business leaders founded the Sierra Club to preserve, enjoy, and explore California's Sierra Nevadas. They elected John Muir to be their first president, a position he held until his death in 1912. The central pillar around which the Sierra Club was structured was: "To explore, enjoy and render accessible the mountain regions of the Pacific Coast; to publish authentic information concerning them; to enlist the support and co-operation of the people and government in preserving the forests and other natural features of the Sierra Nevada."

Outings into the wilderness became an essential part of the club's educational program. Muir firmly believed that the only way to get the American people and their government to protect the American wilderness was to inspire an appreciation through direct contact. In Muir's words, "Few are altogether deaf to the preaching of pine trees. Their sermons on the mountains go to our hearts; and if people in general could be got into the woods, even for once, to hear the trees speak for themselves, all difficulties in the way of forest preservation would vanish." In fact, John Muir personally gave President Theodore Roosevelt a tour of Yosemite

John Muir gazes at a serene view in the Sierra Nevada. Muir believed that the wilderness would make evident its own value if people could be brought to it.

National Park with the hope of winning his support for its preservation.

Ralph Waldo Emerson not only served as an inspiration to John Muir and others but also predicted, in his 1836 essay "Nature," the two predominate conflicting priorities surrounding America's relationship with the environment. First, nature satisfied a utilitarian need for man's shelter, clothing, and food. And second, nature had other "higher" qualities—beauty, language, discipline, moral laws, and spiritual truth. Emerson's conflicting priorities prophetically outline the two attitudes toward the environment that would later divide conservationists. As the transcendentalist Henry David Thoreau remarked after a trip to the Maine woods, "For [every] one that comes with a pencil to sketch or sing, a thousand come with an axe or rifle."

In 1905 these conflicts surfaced when the government presented a plan to dam the Hetch Hetchy Valley of Yosemite National Park to provide water for San Francisco. The ensuing Hetch Hetchy debate served as the catalyst to bring Emerson's two conflicting types of conservation face-to-face.

Gifford Pinchot, a university-trained forester with close ties to political officials, led the group that promoted building the dam and flooding the valley to provide drinking water for San Francisco. Pinchot believed one could scientifically manage forests as consumable resources while conserving their beauty. He championed the science of forestry in America. Pinchot's conservationism accepted the force of progress and the political process. Indeed, he calculated the value of resources in terms of practical and economic criteria and consequently lobbied against the formation of national parks and any other kind of land preservation that would inhibit the commercial use of natural resources. Pinchot espoused conservation as "the greatest good for the greatest number for the longest time."

John Muir spearheaded the opposition group, which sought to preserve Hetch Hetchy in its natural state—virgin territory to remain untouched forever. Muir became the spokesperson for the preservationists. The sensitivity of Muir's writings impressed many of his readers, who believed his works were a veritable gospel of nature. A transcendentalist who knew the wilderness from firsthand experience, he imbued the landscapes of America with an invigorating and spiritual tone. For Muir, the greatest good was to maintain the valley in its untouched splendor, and he blended the intellectual message of the transcendentalists with the urgency and rigor of a religious missionary in his crusade to protect and preserve his beloved mountains. Despite Muir's efforts, Pinchot's voice rang louder in Washington, where legislators were under the influence of industrial constituents.

The utilitarians won the battle, and in 1913, Congress authorized the construction of the dam. John Muir was 75 years old when he lost the battle for Hetch Hetchy. Many feel the loss broke Muir's heart. He died a year later.

With Muir's death, the Sierra Club lost a great leader. But to his honor, the Club continued his work, broadening its focus nationally and internationally.

THE AUDUBON SOCIETY

As industrialization took its toll on the wilderness, the wildlife that depended on wilderness ecosystems suffered. Birds, long used as symbols of freedom, not only fell victim to the ecological strain of urban sprawl but were hunted for their feathers, used to adorn hats and clothing.

In 1883 the American Ornithologists' Union was formed as a citizens' organization to protect game and nongame birds. In 1886, George Bird Grinnell, editor of the sportsman periodical *Forest and Stream*, encouraged his readers to join him in organizing the first bird-preservation organization in the nation. Grinnell named the organization the Audubon Society, after the wildlife artist John James Audubon (1785–1851), who painted life-size portraits of North American birds.

Within a few months, over 30,000 people joined the Audubon Society; it was an immediate success. *Forest and Stream* lacked the financial resources to support the newly formed group, however, and Grinnell was forced to dissolve the society.

Grinnell's short-lived organization inspired many. Mrs. Augustus Hemenway, a prominent Bostonian, decided to form the Boston Audubon Society in 1896. Motivated by her anger at the mass destruction of birds for feathers that adorned ladies' hats, Mrs. Hemenway rallied her high-society friends to boycott hats and clothing decorated with feathers. The boycott brought the club a great deal of publicity. As a result, other local Audubon Societies formed, and within three years there were active societies in 15 states.

The logo of the National Audubon Society.

In 1899, Frank Chapman, an ornithologist at the American Museum of Natural History, began publishing a magazine called *Bird Lore*. Chapman encouraged local Audubon societies to use his magazine to communicate with one another. Two years later, several local clubs formed a loose alliance. And four years later, in New York, this alliance incorporated into the National Association of Audubon Societies for the Protection of Wild Birds and Animals. The association's goal, according to its first president, William Dutcher, was to be "a barrier between wild birds and animals and a very large unthinking class, and a smaller but more harmful class of selfish people." The organization purchased *Bird Lore* from Chapman and made it the official publication of the organization, changing its name to *Audubon Magazine*. The magazine served to unite the members and keep them informed on issues central to the organization.

Audubon members helped inspire and speed the passage of many early conservation laws. In New York, members worked for New York State's Audubon Plumage Law of 1901, which banned the sale of plumes of native New York birds. Audubon members were also influential in the passage of the 1918 Migratory Bird Treaty Act, which instituted federal control of the hunting of migratory birds. The Audubon Society urged the establishment of a national system of wildlife refuge, the first of which was instituted in 1903 on Pelican Island by President Theodore Roosevelt.

The society was equally pioneering in its attempts at environmental education. In 1910, the Audubon Society initiated the first classroom environmental education program with the formation of the Junior Audubon Club. Education, in fact, became a top priority of the Audubon Society. In 1936, the society opened a summer conservation education camp for Junior Audubon Club teachers on Hog Island, Maine. And less than 10 years later, the Audubon Society opened its first education center in Greenwich, Connecticut.

THE IZAAK WALTON LEAGUE

In the late 1800s, diminishing fish counts in rivers and streams prompted scientists, anglers, and other interested citizens to form groups such as the American Fisheries Society, founded in 1870, to protect rivers for fishing. However, these early attempts at waterway protection could not compete with the full-scale assault on the nation's waterways by the many factories that discharged harmful waste directly into streams, rivers, lakes, and oceans. In response, Congress authorized the creation of the U.S. Fish and Fisheries Commission to address the needs of the nation's fishery resources. The commission alone, however, could do little to slow down the attack on the waterways.

In 1922, 54 sportsmen gathered in Chicago, Illinois, outraged at the deteriorating condition of the streams and rivers they fished. They formed an organization called the Izaak Walton League, named after the 16th-century English fisherman, conservationist, and writer Izaak Walton. Walton's book *The Compleat Angler, or the Contemplative Man's Recreation* (1653) espoused the serenity and virtues of nature and outdoor recreation. Just as John Muir looked to Emerson and Thoreau for his spiritual grounding, the Izaak Walton League used the philosophy of Izaak Walton for inspiration.

Two young members of an Audubon youth club in Maine explore the muddy banks of a pond. The Audubon Society and other environmental groups have established educational programs to teach teenagers about the environment.

The league maintained a great affinity with the motivations of hunters, who worked to preserve wilderness areas as a means of ensuring good hunting conditions. "The aims of the league and of local rod and gun clubs are identical," said the league's first president, Will Dilg, "the conservation of our rapidly vanishing outdoor America." The Izaak Walton League's mission today remains true to its original charter: to protect birds, mammals, and fish by saving the nation's threatened wetlands, streams, ponds, and rivers.

From the very beginning, the league accomplished a great deal in the protection of America's waterways and received some patronage from the U.S. government: in 1927 it conducted the nation's first water-pollution survey at the request of President Calvin Coolidge.

The Sierra Club, the Audubon Society, and the Izaak Walton League represent the first tier of environmental action groups. Their hard work and dedication successfully created 13 national parks and 18 national monuments, culminating with the establishment of the U.S. Bureau of National Parks.

In the early conservation groups, several similarities can be identified. First, the fear of not having accessible natural environments for sport and recreation motivated the formation of these groups. Each group emerged in response to the endangerment of a specific natural feature: the mountains for the Sierra Club; birds for the Audubon Society; and fish for the Izaak Walton League. Second, the membership of these early conservation groups consisted for the most part of wealthy and well-educated sportsmen. And finally, the groups informed the public by bringing people directly into natural environments through nature hikes and outdoor expeditions.

Aldo Leopold, pictured here studying the anatomy of birds, helped
found the Wilderness Society in 1934.

PRESERVATION POLITICS

In the first half of the 20th century, American industry boomed as the nation harnessed the potential of her natural resources. World War I (1914–1918), the Great Depression (1929–1939), and World War II (1939–1945) engaged the nation's energies. Environmental efforts were overshadowed by the stark realities of war and poverty. During the Great Depression, the faith of the nation faltered as the promises of capitalism lay unfulfilled. Meanwhile, the demands of war legitimized the gross consumption of natural resources to feed a growing industrial giant.

America emerged from World War II as the most powerful industrial nation in the world. Americans were reeling from the events that had catapulted them into success. The ease and speed of America's transition to world power left the youthful and idealistic nation in a haze of euphoria. As the rest of the world looked on with envy and as Europe began to sweep away the ashes of a ruinous war, America sped into the atomic age. Modernization swept the nation. Science and technology provided new products to a nation obsessed with everything new.

The chemical and plastics industries fed consumers with products of every sort and use, from the practical to the outlandish. It was believed that there was no problem American ingenuity could not overcome and no product that could not be created or improved upon. Farming evolved into a science, and machines, technicians, and economists replaced traditional farmers. It seemed that the American dream was fast becoming a reality.

Hugh Hammond Bennett, the father of soil conservation, recognized in 1939 that Americans, with plowshares and axes, had transformed an untamed wilderness into a mighty, civilized nation. To Bennett, this achievement was a mixed blessing; the taming of forests and streams was destroying the very resources responsible for the nation's success. Bennett saw a direct relationship between the quantity and availability of a nation's natural resources and its standard of living, but he questioned the future availability of resources subject to industrial pressures.

In this new age of abundance, many Americans began to see the need for caution. New conservation groups formed in response to the growing pressures placed on nature by modern industrial society. The Wilderness Society, the National Wildlife Federation, and the Nature Conservancy emerged at this time in response to nature's new aggressors. The fight for conservation broadened from the clubhouse to the statehouse and to courtrooms across America as environmental groups, such as the Environmental Defense Fund, took their cause to the government.

THE WILDERNESS SOCIETY

Aldo Leopold, a Forest Service worker, was an important spokesperson for environmental preservation throughout the

1930s and 1940s. He understood not only the biological and ecological need for preservation but also that America's national character was tied to the experience of taming the wilderness.

Leopold fought for a wilderness-preservation policy within the National Forest System less than a decade after the Hetch Hetchy debates. Like Gifford Pinchot, Leopold had studied forestry. After graduating from college in 1909, Leopold went to work as a forest assistant in the Southwest. While working in Arizona and New Mexico, still territories at that time, he witnessed the diminishing supplies of big game, fish, and fowl in the few untouched wilderness expanses remaining in the country.

In 1913, Leopold came down with a kidney ailment known as Bright's disease. As it had with John Muir, this near brush with death fueled in him a desire to act quickly in defense of the wilderness. Leopold was soon organizing nature-protection groups—first for the protection of game and later for wilderness protection in general. While he is perhaps best known as the author of the book entitled *A Sand County Almanac*, his role as one of the founders of the Wilderness Society was equally influential in promoting the defense of the environment.

Founded in 1935 to help protect the nation's wildlands, the Wilderness Society was conceived by Robert Marshall. Marshall, who came from a wealthy New York family, tried to influence government officials from within their own social circles. Whether working in the Forest Service or the Bureau of Indian Affairs, Marshall persevered with letters, phone calls, and personal visits to other government officials. He knew that the power to protect wilderness lands rested in the hands of the government agencies under whose jurisdiction public lands fell.

Marshall, like Muir, believed in the importance of nature's aesthetic value and often compared scenery of the wilderness to the highest works of art. When asked how many wilderness areas we need, he responded, "How many Brahms symphonies do we need?"

Marshall fully believed that "there is just one hope of repulsing the tyrannical ambition of civilization to conquer every niche on the whole earth. That hope is the organization of spirited people who will fight for the freedom of the wilderness." In 1934 he invited his colleague Leopold and other like-minded preservationists to form a group to preserve the American wilderness from its increasing destruction by the mechanized world. One year later, Marshall gathered the handful of "spirited people" into the Wilderness Society.

Leopold, Marshall, and the other founders of the Wilderness Society were skeptical of the federal government's commitment to wilderness preservation because the government

Robert Marshall at Fairbanks, Alaska, in 1938. Convinced that civilization would conquer "every niche on the whole earth," Marshall conceived of and helped found the Wilderness Society.

was under greater pressure to expand road building, dam construction, and logging. The Wilderness Society was up against great odds, but society members were firm believers in what they collectively called "the gospel of wilderness."

After World War II, the Wilderness Society led the growing national concern for wilderness protection. In its early days, the Wilderness Society never aspired to become a large establishment. Its founding members were entrepreneurs and directors of other conservation organizations—environmental visionaries in their own right. The Wilderness Society grew in size and influence, surpassing the expectations of its founding fathers, with such stunning successes as the passage of the Wilderness Act of 1964.

THE NATIONAL WILDLIFE FEDERATION

Another important organization that emerged during this period was the National Wildlife Federation, founded by Jay Norwood "Ding" Darling, a political cartoonist from Iowa. Darling, in his long career as a conservationist, used the power of words, pictures, and humor to capture the public's attention and win their support.

Darling's outspoken views on conservation led to his 1934 appointment as chief of the Biological Survey, the federal agency responsible for the enforcement of game laws and for overseeing wildlife research. While chief of the Biological Survey, Darling successfully persuaded an irascible judge to rule that "the United States government has a perfect constitutional right to condemn millions of acres for the welfare, health and happiness of ducks, geese, sandpipers, owls and wrens."

Darling's experience at the Biological Survey convinced him that more political action was needed on a federal level if wildlife was to be successfully protected. In 1936, Darling hosted the first North American Wildlife Conference. His keynote address at the conference challenged wildlife organizations to enter the political arena, illustrated how political action worked in our nation's capital, and demonstrated the political ineptitude of conservation organizations: "Our scattered and desultory organizations—36,000 of them—have never, to my certain knowledge, influenced so much as the election of a dog catcher. Thirty-six thousand clubs, leagues, and associations whose chief objective is wildlife conservation. . . . And yet, with all this potential voting strength, the wildlife conservationists together exert less influence on our government, both state and national, than the Barrel-Rollers' Union in Pumpkin Center."

The conference inspired the formation of the General Wildlife Federation, with Darling elected as its president. In 1938 the General Wildlife Federation changed its name to National Wildlife Federation (NWF). The NWF's membership was dominated by sportsmen; the first cash contribution to the organization, in fact, came from the chairman of the Remington Arms Company, the country's largest supplier of hunting ammunition.

The NWF involved itself in legislative efforts from its very beginning. In 1937 the General Wildlife Federation had worked on the Federal Aid in Wildlife Restoration Act, which created an excise tax on firearms to provides states with funds for the preservation of wildlife. In an effort to focus national attention on the constant need for wildlife protection, in 1938 the NWF

President Lyndon Baines Johnson signs the Wilderness Preservation Act, September 3, 1964.

established its "National Wildlife Week" program to expand public awareness. The NWF realized the importance of educating the young on environmental issues. In 1959, the NWF published the children's book *The Adventures of Rick Raccoon.* The book sold 50,000 copies, and the next year it was followed by a sequel, *Ranger Rick and the Great Forest Fire.*

In the early 1960s, inspired by the great success of the Ranger Rick books, the NWF started a monthly magazine called *Ranger Rick.* Ranger Rick became a symbol of the organization's firm belief that young people must be included in its national public awareness program. Through songs, stories, pictures, and rhymes, Ranger Rick brought wilderness conservation to life for many young people in the United States.

In 1962, the National Wildlife Federation began publishing *National Wildlife*, a magazine that targeted two audiences: hunters and fishermen, who wanted the protection of game for recreational purposes, and nonsportsmen interested in general wilderness conservation. Eight years later, the NWF became interested in the international aspects of wildlife protection and began publishing *International Wildlife*.

THE NATURE CONSERVANCY

While some groups were active in the political arena, others were directly purchasing endangered land and wildlife habitats with private funds. The Nature Conservancy formed as the result of a dispute in the Ecological Society of America in 1946 over whether the society should continue with its academic focus or become more active. Those who opted for action forged an organization after the mold of the Nature Conservation, a quasi-governmental organization in Great Britain. Unlike its British role model, the Nature Conservancy became a nongovernmental and nonprofit organization dedicated to purchasing land for preservation.

The Nature Conservancy purchased its first piece of land—60 acres in Mianus River Gorge, New York—for preservation in 1955. Since that first purchase, the Nature Conservancy has pursued its mission to find, protect, and maintain the earth's rare species and natural communities by preserving their natural habitats. The Nature Conservancy has purchased 5.6

million acres for preservation over the years, and today it operates 1,632 wilderness preserves, owns 1.6 million acres of land, and employs nearly 350 scientists to study preservation.

AWAKENING FROM
A SILENT SPRING

Harriet Beecher Stowe's *Uncle Tom's Cabin*, published in 1852, helped to inspire the antislavery movement. Stowe's gripping story argued that blacks were not commodities to be exploited but people deserving the same respect as members of other races. Abraham Lincoln pointed out that Stowe's book was one of the catalysts for the Civil War. One hundred ten years later, another woman, Rachel Carson, wrote a book that would similarly serve as a catalyst for the environmental movement. Carson argued in *Silent Spring* that a living thing, the environment, should not be treated like a disposable commodity.

Silent Spring helped to open the eyes of a nation blindly trusting the promises of the chemical age. In the book Carson showed that the unscrupulous use of pesticides, especially DDT, was not only killing birds and fish but directly threatening the health of humans. Carson argued that all life-forms, even insects, had a valuable place in the cycle of nature. *Silent Spring* was on the *New York Times* best-seller list for over a year, and Carson is credited with making ecology and the environment household words. Carson brought environmental concerns to the forefront of national attention once again, but this time the focus was much broader and the dangers more threatening.

During the 1960s, many new environmental laws were passed, such as the Clean Air Act (1963), the Wilderness Act (1964), and the Endangered Species Act (1966). These laws gave environmentalists a secure footing for further courtroom battles. In addition to already-established wildlife preservation and conservation groups, these new laws prompted the rise of courtroom- and laboratory-oriented environmental groups.

In 1967, a group of people gathered to discuss their concerns over the use of the pesticide DDT on Long Island, New York. From that original meeting, four scientists and an attorney

The Gypsum Dunes Preserve at the foot of the Guadalupe Mountains in Texas is the habitat of several unusual species. The environment is particularly arid, but moisture, needed by certain plants and animals, is stored just below the surface of the dunes.

formed the Environmental Defense Fund (EDF). The organization's goal was to use scientific research to identify and understand environmental problems and the newly established environmental laws to fight in court for environmental cleanup and protection. Within a year, the EDF founders were successful in winning an injunction against DDT spraying in Suffolk County, New York, making the EDF one of the first organizations to employ its own scientific evidence in court. The EDF was not the only organization that formed with the intention of bringing science to the defense of the environment. The Sierra Club Legal Defense Fund and the Natural Resources Defense Council also experienced legislative success, which grew with their means and experience. Court battles with government, industry, and individuals became a viable tool to protect wilderness areas and endangered species, to block dams, to stop or delay the construction of nuclear power plants, and to address other pressing environmental threats.

Spectators at Earth Day 1990 on the Mall in Washington, D.C., play with a beach ball that looks like the earth. The popularity of Earth Day has continued to grow since the first one was held in 1970.

chapter 4

ENVIRONMENTALISM IN THE PUBLIC INTEREST

The 1960s youth culture unabashedly challenged the established political structure and its handling of the Vietnam War and social questions such as civil rights. The euphoric postwar industrial giant began to stumble. Divided over political and social issues, America was thrown into turmoil.

Amid the populist, and often radical, fervor, environmental concerns were addressed with a revitalized sense of urgency. The industrial boom of the 1940s and 1950s left unpredicted chemical pollution of the earth's most basic natural resources: air, water, and soil. The conservation of wilderness areas was overshadowed by more immediate dangers. For the first time people wondered if the nation could alter its course toward destruction, which directly threatened birds, fish, plants, and ultimately humans.

THE NEW SIERRA CLUB

Public reaction to national and international events was partly responsible for the shift of the attitudes and the methods of environmental action groups of the 1960s. Yet these new environmental trends had taken root in the 1950s, by which time many environmentalists were growing weary of conservative (or what they considered to be ineffective) methods. Some new groups were formed, and some simply changed their methods.

In the 1950s, a new generation of leaders brought the Sierra Club to the attention of a broader constituency and paved the way for the action-oriented environmentalism of the following decades. Up to this time, the Sierra Club was best known for its outings into the Sierra Nevada, skiing in the winter and hiking in the spring, summer, and fall. However, the new leadership moved the club to adopt a politically active posture. The youthful new leaders were willing to make wilderness protection their career, not just an avocation. One such leader, photographer Ansel Adams, would become the most well known publicist for the Sierra Nevada through his breathtaking pictures of the region's spectacular beauty.

The greatest influence on the Sierra Club during this period was wielded by David Brower. A native of California, Brower grew up exploring the virgin trails of Yosemite. At the impressionable age of twelve, he read Muir's *My First Summer in the Sierra* and remained for the rest of his life enthralled with the beauty and mystery of the mountains. Brower's love of the mountains led him to become an expert mountain climber, a skill that he taught in Europe during World War II. The condition of the Swiss Alps strengthened his resolve to protect America's wilderness. As Brower explained, "The Alps confirmed my belief in wildness. All those mountains in Switzerland punched so full of holes that they have to be held together with cables. They strengthened my desire to protect the places in the Sierra Nevada."

After the war, Brower, Ansel Adams, and others brought a new spirit to the Sierra Club. They set out to drop the club's gentlemanly approach to wilderness protection, opting for a more aggressive attack on the political machine that was destroying the environment.

In 1952, Brower became the club's first paid executive director; previously its leadership had consisted of amateur conservationists. Shortly after Brower took charge, the club's membership doubled in size, and its budget grew sixfold. The new Sierra Club's first major action was to protest the federal government's plan to build the Glen Echo Dam by flooding Dinosaur National Monument in Utah, which housed a rich deposit of dinosaur skeletons in the remote, wild regions surrounding the Green and Yampa rivers. Prior to the publicity drummed up in response to the plan to flood the region, the monument was virtually unknown to anyone but paleontologists. Conservationists were appalled at the plan not only because it would destroy scenic resources but, more importantly, because it directly threatened the protection and preservation advocated by the national park system.

Conservation groups from many camps launched a political offensive. Few federally elected officials failed to feel the impact of the widespread outrage. Even President Truman received an invitation to raft down the Green River through the national monument. But Truman, in the interests of the economy and powerful industrial lobbyists, continued to press for the dam. The issue was debated on the floor of Congress in 1954 and again in 1955, and Echo Park emerged as the biggest conservation controversy of the decade.

In 1955 the five-year campaign to save Dinosaur National Park ended in a hard-won victory for the environmentalists. The Sierra Club's leadership role in the defeat of the Echo Park Bill spurred the *New York Times* to call the club "the gangbusters of the conservation movement."

After the Echo Park victory, the Sierra Club opposed the Bureau of Reclamation's plan to dam the Grand Canyon. The club wasted no time in bringing national attention to the fight to save the canyon. In an aggressive public-awareness campaign, it placed a full-page advertisement in the *New York Times*,

Two members of the Minnesota Public Interest Research Group man a booth at the 21st annual toy-safety conference. Over the years environmental concerns have broadened to include domestic and occupational environments.

describing the government's plan to dam one of the nation's greatest treasures. The advertisement stated with shocking clarity, "This time it's the Grand Canyon they want to flood. *The Grand Canyon.*"

The stunt succeeded in drawing massive public opposition to the dam. Public officials were flooded with telephone calls and piles of telegrams and letters. Not everyone appreciated this form of lobbying. The day after the advertisement appeared, the Internal Revenue Service (IRS) sent the Sierra Club a letter suspending its tax-exempt status pending a full investigation of the club's political activities. As a not-for-profit organization, the Sierra Club was exempt from paying taxes, and charitable contributions to the organization were tax-deductible. However, this "tax exempt" ruling mandates that an organization refrain from spending an unspecified percentage of its financial resources on lobbying.

This incident marked one of the first times the government had challenged an environmental group's tax-exempt status on the basis of its actions. The Sierra Club, facing a choice between halting its hardball strategy or losing its ability to offer donors tax deductions on their contributions, decided on a third option. It formed separate but related organizations, with different roles and different tax statuses—one conducted direct political lobbying and the other provided noncontroversial public education.

ENVIRONMENTAL ACTION

The new environmental methods appealed to the politically active students of the 1960s. As the Vietnam War escalated, with increased American troop deployment and growing American casualties, student protests opposing the war and demanding social change became more common and more aggressive. One strategy used by student activists and politically concerned professors was the "teach-in." At a teach-in, faculty and students held a loosely structured forum, exchanging information and ideas and venting frustrations about the Vietnam War, civil rights, free speech, and a range of other political and social issues of the day.

In October 1969, in response to growing environmental concerns, Wisconsin senator Gaylord Nelson suggested that Americans set aside April 22, 1970, for a national forum on the environment. Nelson wanted to apply the technique of a teach-in, so popular with the anti–Vietnam War demonstrators, to stimulate the growing war against pollution. The organization Nelson formed to coordinate the event was called Environmental Teach-In Inc.

Nelson offered former Stanford University student body president Denis Hayes the position of national coordinator, setting as his goal "to get a demonstration big enough to force the [environmental] issues into the political dialogue of the country." Hayes jumped at the opportunity, but where Senator Nelson had planned only for a teach-in, Hayes felt that America's youth wanted more. Hayes remarked, "Very early, it was clear to us— and I discussed this with Senator Nelson—that a teach-in was passé. This was not the mood the country was in, to sit in auditoriums and listen. If it was going to be successful, it had to be hands-on, doing something."

Seven months later, on April 22, 1970, the nation held its first and most memorable Earth Day—hailed as the day

This frail-looking tree, engulfed in the towering buildings of Fifth Avenue, was carried through New York City on the first Earth Day in 1970 to plead for the renewal of environmental efforts.

Americans waged war on pollution. Across the nation people joined the festivities. Congress recessed. Four thousand colleges, grade schools, and community groups disseminated environmental information and held informative activities. Politicians and businessmen rushed to podiums and the press, proclaiming themselves environmentalists and trying to garner support from the young and newly political.

People of all ages hoped that the success of Earth Day would be remembered and the promises kept. Legislators offered assurances that government would work to clean up the environment, and business leaders proclaimed their determination to stop industrial pollution and chemical contamination.

But as Earth Day faded into memory, so did its goals and promises. Politicians who had expressed their desire for a clean environment nevertheless voted against meaningful legislation. Industry addressed Earth Day as a public relations affair, not a cost-prohibitive obstacle demanding long-term internal restructuring.

The national organizers of Earth Day saw their work as the beginning of an aggressive campaign, eagerly anticipating a battle in Congress over the Clean Air Act. To their disappointment, they saw none of the established environmental groups poised to fight this battle, so the young groups decided to fight for the legislation. "No environmental group was interested," recalled Hayes. "They were concerned with conservation—birds, wilderness, redwoods." The month before Earth Day, its national organizers had formed a new youth-based group called Environmental Action. The founders of Environmental Action were frustrated by the limited interests of other groups. To the young group, the environment could not be saved without a radical change. They believed that the consumer-oriented economy was responsible for many of the nation's environmental ills. Environmental Action advocated sweeping changes, including recycling, tougher industrial regulations, and a massive educational campaign about particular environmental issues.

Immediately after Earth Day, Environmental Action placed a full-page advertisement in the *New York Times* claiming that "Earth Day Failed" and asking people to join Environmental Action in their environmental work 365 days a year. The advertisement read: "Nearly 20,000,000 people participated in Earth Day. But what did they accomplish? President Nixon proclaimed Boat Week and Archery Week. Politicians came out in favor of clean air, clean water, and apple pie. Corporations said, 'We haven't found the answer to pollution yet. But we're working on it.' And the vast majority of Americans drove to work in their own fumes, ate their daily chemicals and pesticides, discarded millions of tons of junk and wondered why the earth was in such bad shape."

By the first anniversary of Earth Day the painful truth was clear. Few steps had been taken to alleviate pollution. Neither the business community nor the government had increased its attack on environmental problems. It was feared that environmental action groups were the last barrier between pollution and the environment.

Environmental Action saw a possible ally in the fight against environmental destruction in the workers' unions of America. In 1973, Environmental Action worked with the Oil, Chemical, and Atomic Workers union in their boycott against

Hikers pass a hidden lake in the majestic landscape of Mt. Ranier National Park. The pristine beauty of areas like Mt. Ranier and its surroundings inspire many environmentalists to fight for their protec-

Shell products because of the company's refusal to meet worker health and safety demands. The strike ended that summer when Shell finally agreed to listen to workers' concerns about health and safety issues. This strike, for the first time, established occupational health and safety as environmental concerns.

PIRGs

Consumer advocate Ralph Nader once said, "America has more problems than it should tolerate and more solutions than it uses." Nader believed that students had the motivation and ingenuity to find new solutions to the nation's problems. Nader had proved, through his investigations of the automobile industry, that one could fight big business and win. As he said in 1967,

"The question is not whether we can build a car that won't pollute the air. The question is whether we can overcome the resistance of the auto industry and the oil industry to get it built."

Nader and his followers took their tactics to college campuses and set up college-based organizations throughout the country to watchdog industry and government in the public interest. Nader challenged students in the early 1970s to get involved: "Tax yourselves and hire professional staff to help you work on issues of social justice." Students rose to meet his challenge, forming research groups to work for the public interest. These groups became known as public interest research groups (PIRGs). The first PIRG formed at the University of Oregon in 1971, and soon there were PIRGs in California, New York, and New Mexico.

The PIRG formula for action rested on four premises. First, a belief in a personal responsibility for public problems and the welfare of future generations. Second, an emphasis on issues, not candidates. Third, the implementation of pragmatic strategies to bring about social change. And finally, identifying and working toward attainable goals.

By 1990, there were PIRG chapters on roughly 110 campuses in 25 states helping to pass state and federal legislation and keeping a close watch on the environmental policies of government agencies and political officials.

A member of a decontamination and cleanup crew enters a storm sewer in the Love Canal neighborhood of Niagara Falls, New York, where the Hooker Chemical Company buried a toxic waste site that forced citizens to abandon the neighborhood.

chapter 5

THE WAR FOR
THE ENVIRONMENT

The increasingly aggressive environmental defense methods of the 1960s became more common in the 1970s, giving rise to many extremist organizations that took direct action to counter environmental problems. These legal and illegal actions were conducted in protest, with the express purpose of garnering publicity. More aggressive new environmental groups, such as Environmental Action, were reacting to what they saw as the politics of compromise inherent in the lobbyists and legislators of the large, established conservation groups.

Civil disobedience became an increasingly popular tactic among environmentalists. In 1849, Henry David Thoreau said, "If . . . the machine of government . . . is of such a nature that it requires you to be the agent of injustice to another, then, I say, break the law." And indeed, environmentalists took the law into their own hands in efforts to defend the environment. Extreme actions had been taken in the past—in 1889, the mayor of New York ordered workmen to chop down electric and telegraph poles and wires because the utilities company was disregarding the underground burial law—but never with such popularity or on such a grand scale as in the 1970s.

These modern-day "eco-warriors" broke the law in the name of what they considered to be the greater good of protecting the environment. On April 22, 1970, while the rest of the country prepared to celebrate Earth Day, a group calling itself Eco-Commando Force '70 in Dade County, Florida, added yellow dye to the water intake of a sewage treatment plant to test the effectiveness of the system. The next day, half of Dade County's canals turned bright yellow, vividly proving what Eco-Commando Force '70 suspected: the sewage treatment plant was failing to properly process human sewage, which was therefore contaminating local waterways.

Environmental Action approved and publicized this approach of directly alerting the public to environmental dangers. In 1971, Environmental Action launched a nationwide contest for the best antipollution tactics. As Environmental Action explained in Newsweek, "Our senses are dulled to traditional ways of bringing pressure. Conglomerates make labor strikes ineffective and chain stores prevent neighborhood boycotts. Harassment is one of the few catalysts left to make people respond to problems." Environmental Action coined the term "ecotage" (a combination of ecology and sabotage) to describe the tactics employed by "eco-guerrillas" or "ecoteurs." Environmental Action published the most innovative of the ecotage submissions in 1971 in a book entitled Ecotage.

In the vicinity of Ann Arbor, Michigan, a group of students cut down billboards at night. Their ecotage mirrored the pranks described in Edward Abbey's 1975 fictional adventure novel *The Monkey Wrench Gang*, a cult classic that told of a merry band of eco-warriors on a crusade to stop the building of the Glen Canyon Dam in Arizona. In this Robin hood–style environmental adventure, the eco-warriors burn bulldozers, pull up survey stakes that mark new roads, and cut down billboards in acts of defiance against what they consider the evil deeds of developers and politicians.

One of the best-known ecoteurs in the 1970s was the masked man of Kane County, Illinois, called "the Fox." There have been many ecoteurs, but few come close to the Fox's risk-taking exploits. His pranks are legendary among environmentalists. Once, the Fox walked into the headquarters of U.S. Steel and dumped 50 pounds of dead fish and waste effluent on the floor in protest against the company's continued pollution of Lake Michigan. At another time the Fox hung a 60-foot sign from a railroad bridge across the Indiana Toll Road, bearing the message "We're involved—in killing Lake Michigan, signed U.S. Steel." The Fox, with humor and derring-do and by naming specific names, helped expose those responsible for polluting the Midwest. Buttons urging "Bring Back the Fox" can still be found in activist circles.

In response to Greenpeace's efforts to thwart the French government's nuclear testing, two saboteurs, sent by the French government, sunk the Greenpeace vessel Rainbow Warrior while it was docked in Auckland, New Zealand, preparing for further antinuclear activities.

In the 1970s, many environmental action groups adopted the new confrontational methods, but two groups in particular stood out as leaders in the use of these tactics as part of their overall agenda for change: Greenpeace and Earth First! Both formed in the 1970s, and both are as active and as controversial today as they were then.

GREENPEACE

In 1971, a group of citizens of Vancouver, British Columbia, concerned about nuclear-weapons testing, refused to believe the pessimistic saying "There's nothing one person can do." In a small, battered fishing vessel named the *Phyllis Cormack*, twelve men—of which only the captain was an experienced seaman; the rest were journalists, scientists, or activists—departed from a Vancouver dock for the small Alaskan island of Amchitka to block the underground nuclear testing conducted by the U.S. military. The small band called itself Greenpeace.

Greenpeace's mission to save Amchitka was not the first attempt to block nuclear testing in this fashion. Years before, a boat manned by Quakers had set sail for Eniwetok and Bikini on a similar mission, only to be stopped before it ever reached its target. The *Phyllis Cormack* never made it to Amchitka, either, but Greenpeace's attempt to block the test brought international attention to the nuclear testing practices of the U.S. military. As a result of the small, tattered boat's failed—but highly publicized—voyage, public pressure halted all further testing on Amchitka. One year later, the island was turned into a bird sanctuary.

In its first five years, Greenpeace primarily targeted nuclear testing. Several other protest voyages were made—including the highly publicized voyage of the Greenpeace ship *Vega* to block the nuclear atmospheric testing at Mururoa Atoll in French Polynesia—which earned the group its international reputation.

In the late 1970s, Greenpeace broadened its efforts to include the plight of the great whales. Once again, Greenpeace members took to their tattered old boats, this time equipped with inflatable Zodiac motorized rubber rafts, and positioned themselves between the whalers' harpoons and the great sea mammals. The sailors on the whaling ships sprayed the activists with high-pressure water hoses to chase them away from the line of fire, but many whales escaped during the confusion.

Greenpeace's concern for sea mammals then extended to harp seal pups, which are slaughtered for their white pelts. In the frigid Newfoundland winter, Greenpeace volunteers again placed themselves directly between the hunters and the pups. The international attention drawn to the seals by Greenpeace virtually destroyed the market for harp seal pelts, and the yearly slaughter ended.

Greenpeace's relentless direct-action approach on the high seas brought it some enemies as well as admirers. On July 10, 1985, the French government sent special undercover agents to sink the Greenpeace ship *Rainbow Warrior*, docked in New Zealand. In the explosion one person was killed, and the ship sunk. Not only did this action fail to thwart the organization, but over the next few years Greenpeace expanded to land-based activities as well.

To fight environmental injustice on land, Greenpeace used elaborate stunts to draw media attention and bring their message to the general public. They became notorious for hanging giant banners off the most precarious but highly visible places. Greenpeace activists climbed the scaffolding around the Statue of Liberty as it was being renovated and hung a massive banner on it that bore the message "Give me liberty from nuclear weapons. Stop testing." And when a barge loaded with Philadelphia's garbage could not find a place to unload its cargo and was docked off the Atlantic shore, Greenpeace climbed aboard the barge and spread a banner across the front reading "Next time try recycling."

On land or at sea, Greenpeace has commanded the attention of the world with its popular stunts. Today Greenpeace is one of the largest environmental organizations in the world, with offices on almost every continent, including Antarctica.

EARTH FIRST!

Perhaps the most controversial environmental action group is Earth First! Whether an Earth First! member is suspended

Greenpeace members salute with gestures of peace and defiance aboard the Phyllis Cormack, *which is bound for the Alaskan island of Amchitka to attempt to block underground nuclear testing conducted by the U.S. military.*

from a giant redwood tree in an old-growth forest to protest against logging or sings songs about how to sabotage bulldozers at land-development sites, Earth First! walks the finest line between legal and illegal environmental protest. And yet such an extremist organization makes the concerns and proposals of the more traditional groups seem more reasonable and more acceptable to industry and legislators.

Why did Dave Foreman, Earth First!'s founder, think the environmental movement needed such a group? Foreman, a onetime farrier from New Mexico, served as the Wilderness Society's chief lobbyist in Washington, D.C., in the late 1970s. From his experience in the nation's capital, he concluded that it is useful to "have a group to take a tougher position than the Sierra Club and the Wilderness Society." This band of extremists would serve to move the center position between "reasonable" and "unreasonable" environmental demands closer to the environmentalists' ultimate goals by making other environmental groups look more conservative.

Foreman's idea became a reality shortly after he left the Wilderness Society in 1979. On a trip with four friends in the Pinacate Desert, Mexico, Foreman shared his vision of forming a group dedicated to taking a noncompromising position on environmental-protection issues. The five agreed that the earth must come first. Drawing on the environmental philosophy of John Muir and Aldo Leopold and using the role model of monkey wrenching as their organizational strategy, the five cemented the foundation for Earth First!

Within a short time of its founding, Earth First! developed its own techniques of monkey wrenching, such as putting an ostentatious crack in Glen Canyon Dam by lowering a long,

These eco-commandos hang from an autobahn bridge over the Rhine in Germany, blocking ship traffic to protest against the pollution of the river.

zigzagged piece of black plastic down the dam's concrete front wall. Foreman proclaimed, "The finest fantasy of eco-warriors in the West is the destruction of [Glen Canyon] Dam and the liberation of the Colorado [River]."

One characteristic feature of Earth First! is its loose organizational structure: no officers and no official offices. Members spread the organization's message by giving "road shows," a combination of music and speeches that proclaim the message: "No compromise in defense of mother earth."

By the mid-1980s, Earth First! had wrapped its offensive strategy in the philosophical concepts of Deep Ecology, which asserts that all living things on the planet are worth defending. In other words, a two-month-old grizzly bear cub and a 200-year-old Sequoia redwood deserve as much respect as a human being. Moreover, Deep Ecology summoned those who felt likewise to action. Action became the hallmark of Earth First! In *Ecodefense*, Earth First!'s manual on monkey wrenching, Foreman wrote, "Go out and *do* something. Pay your rent for the privilege of living on this beautiful, blue-green, living Earth. Monkey wrenching will succeed as a strategic defense of the wild only if it is enthusiastically and joyously undertaken by many individuals in many places."

A routine day at the office is disturbed by two plucky Greenpeace members who are hanging a banner to protest the use of poisonous chemicals in the manufacture of paper. The toxins are often discarded in an irresponsible manner and spread through rivers and lakes.

A local chapter of Friends of the Earth gather to protest the general lack of motivation for environmental causes. The sign on the right reads: "Work, Consume, Be Silent, Die. I Rely on Your Apathy. It's Costing the Earth."

By the late 1980s, Earth First! had entered into wilderness disputes all over the West. In the battle to protect old-growth forests in northern California, Earth First! member's sat on platforms suspended from trees in the threatened old-growth forests for several days so that the loggers could not work without injuring the activists. A similar tactic, supposedly employed by Earth First!, that has generated great controversy and unfavorable publicity is tree spiking. This is the practice of driving a metal spike into a threatened tree as a deterrent to loggers, who avoid spiked trees so as not to catch their chain saws on the spikes. In

1987, a worker at a sawmill was injured when a band saw hit a spiked log. Much controversy exists surrounding this incident; however, no group or individual has ever been charged with a criminal offense.

On the high seas, Foreman's call to action was answered by a group called Sea Shepherd. Paul Watson, international director of Sea Shepherd, sees a close relationship between the work of his organization and the work of Earth First! "We are the navy to Earth First!'s army. It's the war to save the planet. This kind of action will be getting stronger. The environmental movement doesn't have many deserters and has a high level of recruitment. Eventually there will be open war."

This button with its antinuclear slogan adorns the coveralls of a protester in Washington, D.C. The slogan is a takeoff of the anti–Vietnam War slogan "Hell No! We won't go!"

chapter 6

" H E L L   N O !
W E   W O N ' T   G L O W ! "

Existing environmental organizations address new problems as they arise, or altogether new groups form. Advances in technology have complicated environmental efforts. Chemical manufacturers often use and disseminate chemical products and their wastes before the dangers of the chemicals are known. Legislative efforts to test and control new technology cannot possibly keep pace with the efforts of scientists and researchers working for lucrative industrial firms. And war often places deadlines on technology as scientists work feverishly to devise diabolic new weapons to speed the war to an end. This was the case with the development of the atomic bomb. The splitting, and eventually the fusing, of atomic nuclei, which produces tremendous bursts of radioactive energy, inspired the formation of new environmental groups that fought to stop the possible horrors of nuclear war or of a nuclear accident.

Though united by the common goal of eliminating the nuclear threat, antinuclear establishments are as disparate in form and method as groups from the entire history of the nonnuclear environmental movement. Antinuclear efforts began with the very scientists who unlocked the power of the atom. These scientists formed the first antinuclear organization in 1945, the Federation of Atomic Scientists. Later, scientists joined other politically active organizations, such as the National Committee for a Sane Nuclear Policy, which shortly thereafter became known simply as SANE. From the 1950s through the 1980s, SANE presented sobering information about the insanity of nuclear armament. And in the midst of the turbulence of the 1960s, college professors at the Massachusetts Institute of Technology (MIT) formed the Union of Concerned Scientists to promote the peaceful and progressive use of education and research for the social welfare of the nation; in other words, scientific research for peace, not war.

Students, on the other hand, frustrated with the tactics of the early antinuclear organizations, formed their own campus-based antinuclear groups, and citizens living near proposed or existing nuclear power plants also joined together in opposition to the facilities. All of these groups sought to draw public attention to the possible effects of an atomic accident.

And out of this eclectic collection of environmental action groups came a national awareness of the environmental consequences of nuclear energy and nuclear war.

FEDERATION OF ATOMIC SCIENTISTS AND THE BULLETIN OF ATOMIC SCIENTISTS

Young scientists working in the Metallurgy Laboratory of the Manhattan Project, the government's operation to develop the atomic bomb, formed the Federation of Atomic Scientists in 1945 and published the *Bulletin of Atomic Scientists* to vent their opinions.

The challenge of unraveling the secrets of nature had inspired these young scientists to harness the power of the atom.

But when they saw the cataclysmically destructive properties of their own discoveries, a solemn consciousness swept the scientific community.

The image of mushroom clouds rising over the Japanese cities of Hiroshima and Nagasaki, the result of the atomic bombs dropped by the U.S. military in 1945, haunted the scientists. When the mushroom clouds settled, the scientists read reports and saw photos of the bomb's aftermath—flattened cities, charred bodies, and ghoulishly disfigured survivors. The dropping of the atomic bombs helped speed World War II to an end, but the young scientists were left with an ominous burden on their conscience.

"The atom bomb is a Pandora's box," said physicist Eugene Rabinowitch. "We helped open that box and as scientists have a responsibility to humanity to tell the world what we know about this monster."

The scientists of the Manhattan Project, previously separated from one another and sworn to secrecy, organized themselves into a number of groups to discuss the implications of their work. The scientists believed that they must take

People of all ages have taken up the fight for a nuclear-free world. This woman looks for antinuclear sentiment among local motorists.

responsibility for their actions, even against the wishes of the federal government.

In November 1945, the Manhattan Project scientists met at the University of Chicago "to promote the use of scientific discoveries in the interest of world peace and the general welfare of mankind." A group of atomic scientists at the University of Chicago spearheaded the formation of a federation that would unite the small groups of scientists and provide mutual aid and support for all atomic scientists at laboratories scattered across the country. The Federation of Atomic Scientists was the result.

Two physicists in the Chicago group of scientists decided to publish a newsletter, the *Bulletin of Atomic Scientists*, to inform the public and politicians about the dangers of nuclear energy, including the horrifying consequences of nuclear war. Shortly thereafter, the journal became the official voice of the Federation of Atomic Scientists. The purpose of the *Bulletin*, as stated in its founding constitution, was twofold:

1. To explore, clarify and formulate the opinion and responsibilities of scientists in regard to the problems brought about by the release of nuclear energy, and

2. To educate the public to a full understanding of the scientific, technological and social problems arising from the release of nuclear energy.

Meeting in basement classrooms and at coffee shops, the scientists worked to make the *Bulletin* a vehicle by which to convey knowledge of nuclear science and technology to the layperson. The atomic scientists believed such information was essential to democratic decision making in the atomic age.

The federation believed that if they informed the public and the politicians about the ghastly dangers inherent in the atomic bomb—knowledge they had gained from participation in its construction—worldwide safety precautions would result.

A clock poised, ready to strike the midnight hour, indicating the need to address atomic questions before time runs out, became the logo of the *Bulletin*. In 1947, the clock read seven minutes to midnight. By 1949 the clock had moved to three minutes to midnight with the detonation of the first Soviet atomic bomb. The clock moved forward and backward as hopes of peace rose and fell during the Cold War. In 1992, after the disintegration of the Soviet Union and the fall of communism in Eastern Europe, the *Bulletin*'s famous clock stopped and then began ticking again, this time for world peace.

Why did the scientists feel compelled to speak out and stand against nuclear weapons? Albert Einstein, in a speech at a Nobel anniversary dinner in New York, explained: "Physicists find themselves in a position not unlike that of Alfred Nobel. Alfred Nobel invented an explosive more powerful than any then known—an exceedingly effective means of destruction. To atone for this 'accomplishment' and to relieve his conscience he instituted his award for the promotion of peace. Today, the physicists who participated in producing the most formidable weapon of all time are harassed by a similar feeling of responsibility, not to say guilt. As scientists, we must never cease to warn against the danger created by these weapons."

In June 1957, 27 influential citizens met in New York City and started a group they called the Provisional Committee to Stop Nuclear Tests. By the autumn of that year the committee had blossomed into a larger organization and adopted the name National Committee for a Sane Nuclear Policy—SANE for short.

"SANE was founded on the basic liberal premise that mistaken U.S. policies can be remedied and set right; and that in order to do so, the imperatives are effective communication, dialogue, public education, and direct political action," wrote SANE historian Milton Katz. Unlike many environmentally minded organizations, SANE worked within the system, frowning on tactics such as civil disobedience, marches, and ecotage.

The founders of SANE included members of the Federation of Atomic Scientists and activists in the world government movement. As one SANE leader explained, "The need for world government was clear long before August 6, 1945, but Hiroshima and Nagasaki raised that need to such

Militants of the environmental group Greenpeace display a "stop plutonium" banner on a crane in the military port of Cherbourg, in western France, to protest the arrival of a Japanese freighter loaded with 1.7 tons of plutonium.

dimensions that it can no longer be ignored." The world-government movement advocated the establishment of the United Nations.

SANE's founding chairmen were Norman Cousins of the *Saturday Review* and Clarence Pickett of the American Friends Service Committee. SANE's first action was to publish a stark message in the *New York Times* in 1957 that warned, "We are facing a danger unlike any danger that has ever existed."

SANE worked to shape public policy through lobbying and public-information campaigns. Speeches and high-visibility advertisements garnered the attention of the general public and the press. Moreover, SANE's well-connected membership granted it access to influential public officials.

SANE's accomplishments included organizing some of the largest antinuclear rallies of the 1950s and 1960s. In 1965, SANE sponsored the largest antiwar rally to date. By the 1970s, SANE's accomplishments included leading the fight against the proposed antiballistic missile (ABM) system, the B-1 bomber, and the MX missile. SANE's members also aided in the passage of the Strategic Arms Limitation Treaty (SALT).

UNION OF CONCERNED SCIENTISTS

With the Federation of Atomic Scientists as their role model, faculty at MIT formed the Union of Concerned Scientists (UCS) in 1969 in response to the Vietnam War. The organization's founding statement began, "Misuse of scientific and technical knowledge presents a major threat to the existence of mankind." The group of scientists asserted that scientific research conducted at universities should not be used to benefit the military but for solving environmental and social problems. The UCS members called on their colleagues at MIT and other universities to join them in actively working toward "a more responsible exploitation of scientific knowledge."

The UCS published reports and conducted studies on nuclear power and weapons technology. The goals of the Union of Concerned Scientists consisted of nuclear arms reductions, a sensible and stabilizing national security policy, nuclear power safety, and a sound energy policy for the nation. In 1972, the UCS provided important technical testimony at national hearings on the safety and adequacy of the emergency core-cooling systems operating at nuclear power plants. Their findings revealed failures in the system as well as blatant negligence in safety and operations by the nuclear-power industry. These findings sparked broad public concern over the safety of nuclear power.

THE CLAMSHELL ALLIANCE

One of the model grass-roots antinuclear groups formed in the 1970s was the Clamshell Alliance. Though not the first group opposed to the construction of a nuclear power plant in Seabrook, New Hampshire, the Clamshell Alliance provided a model for the organizational structure of later groups.

Opposition to the plant was voiced as early as 1969, when the site was first acquired by the New Hampshire Public Service Company. Concern over the proposed construction of the Seabrook nuclear power plant instigated immediate lobbying and lawsuits in an attempt to halt its construction.

In April 1976, frustration with the lack of success of these tactics led to a strictly nonviolent protest rally. The rally received a favorable reaction from most of the surrounding communities and the press, but the Nuclear Regulatory Commission (NRC) nevertheless issued the utilities company a temporary construction permit two months later. Leaders of a variety of environmental action groups fighting the proposed plant shortly thereafter formed a coalition that became the Clamshell Alliance, so named because the Seabrook plant encompasses a saltwater estuary rich in clams. Many in the town of Seabrook made their living by clamming.

Recognizing the failures of earlier efforts, especially in the courts, to stop the plant, the Clamshell Alliance employed mass civil disobedience. Demonstrators protested on the site, illegally occupying the plant. They claimed that since radioactivity would know no boundaries in trespassing against humanity, they, too, would trespass, in the name of humanity. These high-profile actions alerted the public to the possible calamities of nuclear power—problems that could arise from improper construction, faulty safety features, or human error. An early Clamshell Alliance slogan read: "Better Active Today Than Radioactive Tomorrow." And the Clamshell Alliance's actions successfully drew public support and participation.

Why did people get involved? According to Gunter, "Many originally got involved out of a gut-level reaction. They knew that the promise of power 'too cheap to meter' didn't sound right." The promise of cheap energy was not enough to endanger the existence of every living thing in the region.

Other groups modeled themselves on the Clamshell Alliance, such as the Abalone Alliance in California, the Conch

Shell Alliance in Florida, and the Shad Alliance on Long Island. But what did these groups accomplish?

When the Clamshell Alliance was founded, the U.S. government wanted to construct one thousand nuclear power plants by the year 2000. After the efforts of antinuclear groups, hundreds of reactors were canceled during construction, and even more were scratched in the planning stage. Delays in the construction of reactors caused by the activists undermined the confidence of investors. By 1992, just eight years from the government's target date for the completion of 1,000 nuclear power plants, only 112 reactors were in operation, with no plans for new reactors.

PEACE CAMPS

The NATO decision to deploy a new arsenal of U.S nuclear missiles in Western Europe inspired a new type of antinuclear demonstration. One of the bases chosen to house this arsenal was the U.S. air base at Greenham Common, west of London.

In 1981, as preparations for the new missiles proceeded, forty British women walked the 120 miles from Wales to Greenham Common to protest the new nuclear missile site. The news media ignored the march. Not to be stopped or silenced by the press blackout, the women stayed at the base in protest. Their spontaneous action gave birth to the Greenham Common women's peace camp.

At first, the goal of the Greenham Common peace camp was to bring public attention to, and spark public debate over, the deployment of nuclear weapons. As days turned to weeks and weeks turned to months and the protesters held out, the peace camp became a full blockade of any new nuclear missiles entering the base.

The peace camp drew a constant influx of women supporters, allowing the participants to come and go as necessary without breaking the camp's solidarity. The press, both in London and around the world, could no longer ignore the protesters, and the peace camp became front-page news. Even though cruise missiles entered the base two years later, the camp, continuing its nonviolent resistance, was considered a success.

Inspired by the Greenham Common women, peace camps sprang up at nuclear-weapons installations around the Western world. In July 1984, thousands of women converged on the Seneca Army Depot in Seneca Falls, New York, to protest America's first European deployment of a first-strike arsenal of cruise and Pershing II missiles.

The Seneca Falls protest began as a march to the depot, but once at the depot gate, some women joined in an unchoreographed dance simulating nuclear-holocaust victims, culminating with each dancer falling to the ground, dead from the nuclear ordeal. Around the dancers, other women decorated the fence surrounding the installation with messages of peace, pictures of their children, and flowers. Each item served to transform the fence from a lifeless barrier against intrusion to a lively ornamented collage.

Billie Kahn, a women who took part in the Seneca Falls march and encampment, found herself humbled by the courage and untiring passion for peace of the women around her. She wrote, "If there is to be a future, it will be because of people like them. Does what they do make a difference to the men in Washington and Moscow? I don't know. I can only hope so."

McDonald's, which has always been popular with young people, was picketed because of the restaurant chain's use of styrofoam cups and containers, which are made with CFCs that damage the earth's protective ozone layer. McDonald's has since switched to paper products.

chapter 7

GRASS-ROOTS ENVIRONMENTALISM

In the late 1970s and early 1980s, a series of tragedies struck communities affected by environmental pollution. It seemed that industry was simply producing too much waste to store in a safe manner, so it began illegally dumping as dusty environmental bills sat on the back shelves of congressional offices. One such disaster occurred in a section of Niagara Falls, New York, known as Love Canal.

The Hooker Chemical Company had buried a large quantity of toxic waste in the neighborhood of Love Canal. To dispose of the mess and escape legal responsibilities, the company sold the site to the local school board for one dollar. The school board was aware of the waste, supposedly stored in safe barrels beneath the topsoil, but the price was too tempting. The board then built a school directly on top of the waste site. After a short time, complications arose. At night the playground glowed with a ghastly greenish hue, and children returned from school with mysterious rashes and other medical complaints.

In 1978, Lois Gibbs, a mother and resident of Love Canal, read an article in the local paper that identified an abandoned chemical dump underneath her neighborhood. From this article she learned that many chemicals supposedly in the waste site caused the same illnesses plaguing her young son Michael. Every day, Michael played on the school grounds, directly on top of the chemical waste.

Gibbs questioned local residents and learned from other mothers of their sick children. She went to Michael's school and asked to have him transferred. The principal told her bluntly, "I'm not going to transfer a child because of one hysterical housewife. If I did that, I'd be admitting there was a problem." Gibbs was not discouraged. She decided that if he refused to do anything for one parent, perhaps he might act if a large number of parents started asking questions and demanding action.

Gibbs and her neighbors formed the Love Canal Home Owners Association (LCHA), with Gibbs elected president. The LCHA sought answers to the mysteries hovering about the abandoned chemical site. What chemicals lurked below? What were the health effects of these chemicals? How could the site be cleaned up? Who would pay the costs of the cleanup?

When the community realized that the canal could not be cleaned up fast enough to protect their immediate health, they fought for relocation. The residents asked the government to buy their homes, now worthless because of the contamination. In a united effort to bring state and national attention to their plight, many in the community, from grandparents to grade-school children, joined the LCHA's public pressure campaign. They picketed the mayor's office and the governor's office. They even followed President Jimmy Carter's reelection campaign around the country with signs asking "What are you going to do about Love Canal?" Their persistence paid off. In 1980, President Carter signed an agreement with the state of New York to buy all the homes in Love Canal, enabling the residents to relocate.

By the early 1980s, it became apparent that there were environmental problems in every state, every county, and perhaps every town—the Stringfellow acid pits in Riverside, California, the dioxin contamination at Times Beach, Missouri, the PCB (polychlorinated biphenyl) contamination in Bloomington, Indiana, and many more.

The EPA's national priorities list for the cleanup of the nation's worst hazardous-waste sites in 1980 included hundreds of locations. Today the number is estimated in the tens of thousands, and even that may be a conservative estimate. Environmental crises exist in greater numbers than ever imagined, and communities are organizing to protect themselves as best they can.

From her involvement with the Love Canal crisis, Lois Gibbs learned that citizens could make a difference. She decided to relocate to Arlington, Virginia, and start a national grass-roots environmental crisis center named Citizens' Clearinghouse for Hazardous Waste (CCHW). Gibbs remembers the founding of CCHW: "In 1981, I started CCHW in the basement of my new home in Arlington, VA. I was broke and so was CCHW. I wanted to share what we had learned so other people could fight for themselves and win. I also wanted to fill a big gap—we set up CCHW to be the kind of group I wish I could have called when I first got started at Love Canal."

People from all over the country called Gibbs and said things like "We think we've got a Love Canal in our backyard. What should we do?" In many ways, the Love Canal incident was just one of many environmental crises popping up at an alarming

These grandmothers protest against the proliferation of nuclear warheads in Europe. The nuclear missiles, they claim, are intended for first strikes, not defense.

rate. But many communities followed the example of the LCHA and organized their own grass-roots action groups.

One of these groups was the National Toxics Campaign (NTC). The NTC is part of a coalition of consumer organizations, environmental groups, farmers, lawyers, businessmen, public health officials, scientists, and educators working to develop citizen-based solutions to the nation's environmental problems. Headquartered in Boston, the NTC hires local activists to help establish or stimulate grass-roots environmental groups in other areas.

A 1983 article in the *Chicago Tribune* documenting the rise of grass-roots environmentalism described their actions and motivation as follows: "Theirs is a guerrilla war waged from door to door in the communities across America. Their only weapons against the cool discipline of scientists and the frequent callousness of public officials are passion, placards and public opinion. They believe they are fighting, actually, for their lives."

The discovery that hazardous chemical wastes have been dumped near their homes binds them together with the fear that they and their children are slowly being poisoned by the refuse of an industrial society.

They appeal for answers, answers that often don't exist, in an emotional crusade that turns housewives into community organizers and their children into television stars. They plot strategy over coffee in the kitchen and besiege bureaucrats with pleas for help in the belief that if they make enough noise, someone will notice.

Industry called groups opposed to industrial dumping in their communities NIMBYs, an acronym that stands for "Not in My Backyard." Industry had long been weaving through the loopholes of environmental law. But the NIMBY citizen action groups presented a new obstacle to the cheap dumping of industrial waste.

One such NIMBY group is People Against Hazardous Landfill Sites (PAHLS). PAHLS is a grass-roots organization formed in 1981 to fight a 125-acre landfill in Wheeler, Indiana—a small rural town of 500 people made up of family farmers and blue-collar steel-mill workers. As Sue Greer, the executive director of PAHLS, recalls, "At first, PAHLS members knew nothing about landfills, hazardous waste, or groundwater contamination; none of our original members had a college education. But because this was our town, our farms, and our families, we got involved. We started educating ourselves and the community about landfills and pollution."

By picketing, protesting, and an unflagging determination, the citizens of Wheeler convinced the landfill owner, Waste Management Inc., to withdraw its application for a permit to dump hazardous waste in their town. News of PAHLS's success spread, inspiring other communities throughout northwest Indiana with similar problems to contact PAHLS for advice about their environmental problems. "We helped them realize that if we

When President George Bush refused to sign significant portions of the international environmental agreements at the Rio Earth Conference in 1992, many Americans were outraged.

could do it, they could too. And if they could do it, so could others," said Sue Greer. "The corporate polluters had pushed us around long enough. By organizing we started pushing back."

Whereas PAHLS formed to block chemical dumping in a landfill, the Coalition for Health Concerns, in Benton, Kentucky, formed to investigate the possible link between the town's unusually high cancer rate and its local factories. The severity of the situation struck Corrine Whitehead, a Benton resident, during Christmas of 1984. "That Christmas a couple that had been friends of mine for many years were both in the hospital with cancer. After seeing many husbands and wives succumbing to cancer and then seeing it be someone close to me, it made me do something."

Whitehead's first action was to search for more information. As the land-use chair of the Kentucky League of Women Voters, she arranged a public forum on hazardous waste. She called the Tennessee Valley Authority (TVA) in search of a speaker. The TVA said they would not only provide a speaker but would also release the findings of their regional study on hazardous waste to Whitehead and cosponsor the meeting.

The TVA report revealed that the Calvert City area had the highest concentration of toxins in the state. Over a hundred people attended the public program, and out of that meeting in 1985 came the formation of the Coalition for Health Concerns (CHC), with Whitehead at the helm.

The founding mission of the CHC was to find the potential causes of illness in the community. "Many of our members are cancer victims," says Whitehead. "It's always been a victim's organization." The CHC identified the link between the illnesses suffered in their community and exposure to the industrial discharges of toxic materials from local factories.

Both PAHLS and the CHC remain active today. Both have won small victories—shutting down a smokestack or cleaning up a contaminated site—but the strength of these organizations is in their number. In many cities, towns, and counties similar groups exist battling polluters on a local level. Women like Gibbs, Greer, and Whitehead, who have been called "hysterical housewives" by some, recognize that their perseverance has improved life in their communities and perhaps even saved lives.

Where conservation groups seek to protect and preserve nature in its pristine form, and its inhabitants, grass-roots community environmentalism engages in the self-preservation of humankind—the desire for toxin-free air, water, and land.

Union members take to Central Park in New York City to protest against nuclear testing and to call for nuclear disarmament.

Female members of the Student Environmental Action Coalition express their environmental concerns at a women's rally. Students have consistently been the most active supporters of environmental causes.

chapter 8

MAKING   EVERY   DAY   EARTH   DAY

The United Nations Conference on Environment and Development (UNCED), commonly called the Rio Earth Conference, in Rio de Janeiro, Brazil, June 1992, brought together political leaders from around the world to discuss global environmental problems. The mission of the UNCED was to open international dialogue on environmental protection. Two historic treaties were signed at the conference, one on global warming and the other a broad outline to preserve the planet's natural resources. Alongside the official UNCED events, an international gathering of nongovernmental organizations (NGOs) held their own nonpolitical, populist summit on the environment. The NGOs, meeting outside the official summit halls, presented a bleaker picture of the global environmental landscape, asserting that contaminated water and polluted air respect no political borders and that environmental pollution poses a threat to worldwide health and economic stability.

At the unofficial summit, concerned citizens from nations across the globe exchanged stories of oozing waste sites, blackened skies, and vanishing animal species. If the politicians could not work fast enough, they were determined to take action, and ideas were exchanged among participants in an atmosphere of solidarity.

The most visible recent emergence of environmental awareness has come from the former Soviet-bloc countries. Because of the disregard for environmental concerns during Communist rule, Eastern Europe is cursed with some of the most polluted regions on the planet. The fight for political freedom has inspired an activist spirit that has quickly spread to the environment. For example, in Bulgaria in 1989 a small group formed to protect the Russe region from industrial degradation. Within a year the group, called Ecoglasnost, became a voice for many of the environmental concerns in Bulgaria. Today the group functions as both a political and an environmental organization.

With the opening, called perestroika, of the former Soviet Union in the 1980s to outside ideas, a new cooperation among nature preservationists and environmentalists spread throughout the former republics. The Socio-Ecological Union (SEU) was established in 1988 to unify ecology groups on city and regional levels. In 1990 the SEU, along with the American organization Institute for Soviet American Relations (ISAR), held the Soviet Union's first nongovernmental environmental conference, with representatives from all of the republics, to discuss environmental problems, concerns, and possible solutions. With the fall of Communist rule and the birth of independent republics, the SEU continues to function as a conduit of information for the entire region.

In the United States many international environmental groups exist. Some such groups focus their efforts on a specific region of the world. For example, the African Wildlife Foundation, based in Washington, D.C., is an international organization

At the United Nations Conference on Environment and Development in Rio de Janeiro, Brazil, Archilles Karamanlis, the Greek minister for the environment, prepares to sign the Convention on Biological Diversity.

working to protect African wildlife. The foundation provides funding and technical training for African-based preservation groups, thus using financial resources from the United States to train local Africans to defend and preserve their own wildlife.

Other American-based international organizations focus on particular issues rather than specific geographic areas. The Rainforest Action Network, founded in 1985 in San Francisco, California, works to publicize the destruction of tropical rain forests and the plight of those living in the forests. The Rainforest Action Network consists of over 150 rainforest action groups nationwide. Through newsletters and public forums, each group encourages its members to promote an understanding of the gravity of the present situation.

A third type of American-based international environmental organization functions as a communications and logistics center for an international network of local groups. The most prominent group of this type is Friends of the Earth (FOE). FOE was founded by David Brower in 1969 after he left the Sierra Club. Brower believed that environmental protection would ultimately depend on international efforts and cooperation. Now in its 27th year, FOE has nongovernmental affiliates in 42 countries.

One such FOE affiliate is Red di Ecologia Social
(REDES)—the Social Ecological Network—of Uruguay. REDES
was founded in 1989 as a member group of FOE International.
From its earliest days, REDES recognized a direct relationship
between environmental and social problems. For example, one
of REDES's campaigns is the Eco-Community Project in the
economically ravaged Montevideo district. Many people in this
district live by collecting garbage alongside the watershed.
Alberto Villareal, the coordinator of the project, believes that a
close connection exists between environmental, social, and
psychological problems. In an interview published in the book
*Earth Summit: Conversations with Architects of an Ecologically
Sustainable Future*, Villareal stated that "part of the work in this
project has to do with cleaning up the water sheds and basins
from contamination. But a lot of it is social work as well helping
to find environmental and socially appropriate solutions with and
for the people living on them and it is very hard work. Living as
these people do in a very deprived situation easily generates
psychosocial pathologies that are difficult to deal with."

In 1990, FOE absorbed the Oceanic Society and the
Environmental Policy Institute, becoming an organization that

*At an environmental rally
in Washington, D.C., the
environmental group
Friends of the Earth in-
flated a monstrous earth
balloon to attract people
to their information booth.*

could address a broader set of problems. FOE describes itself as a "global advocacy organization that works at local, national and international levels to: protect the planet; preserve biological, cultural and ethnic diversity; and empower citizens to have a voice in decisions affecting their environment and lives."

There is a Native American saying "We don't inherit the earth from our parents. We borrow it from our children." Many young people are active in the environmental movement in America and abroad. In the former Soviet Union, one of the older and more active preservation societies is a student group. In the former Soviet Union, the student ecological movement started in 1950 under the name Druzhini, "Lifeguard of Nature." Throughout its history, Druzhini has helped establish over 200 different nature reserves and encouraged four decades of urban youth to appreciate the environment.

Student environmental groups are growing in popularity in the United States. One of the largest and most active is the Student Environmental Action Coalition (SEAC). SEAC was founded in 1988 by students at the University of North Carolina at Chapel Hill. Originally called the Society of Environmentally Concerned Students, the organization changed its name and began working jointly with students at neighboring Duke University on the issue of the Arctic National Wildlife Refuge.

Inspired by the success of and enthusiasm of the student population for the joint project, SEAC placed a small announcement in *Greenpeace* magazine explaining their purpose and soliciting new members. Over 200 student groups responded.

The following year, SEAC held a conference to bring together student groups from campuses across the country. An overwhelming 1,700 students attended the SEAC Threshold

Seven-year-old Russell Essary, concerned about the depletion of the ozone layer and global warming, organized the environmental action group Kids STOP.

Conference. The conference helped solidify a nationwide network of college-based environmental groups, with SEAC-UNC serving as the national coordinating body. Over the next six months, newly formed SEAC chapters held marches and rallies in support of environmental concerns, from saving the Arctic National Wildlife Refuge to avoiding hazardous-waste sites in their community.

In 1990, SEAC held its second national conference in Champaign, Illinois. The Catalyst Conference brought together 7,600 students from all 50 states and from over 10 countries. Out of this conference SEAC's second national campaign emerged, focusing on corporate accountability. SEAC now has over 1,500 chapters on high school and college campuses.

Even younger people have made a difference. In the fall of 1989, Russell Essary, age seven, of Forest Hills, New York, started asking his parents questions about global warming and the depletion of the ozone layer. After some research, he and his parents came to the conclusion that automobile air-conditioner repairs contribute significantly to the amount of chlorofluoro-carbons (CFCs) being released into the atmosphere. Russell decided to do something about it. He organized his friends into a group calling itself Kids STOP. With letters and testimony, Kids STOP pressured the local city council to pass a resolution banning the release of CFCs into the atmosphere during auto repairs. Kids STOP succeeded in getting the resolution passed, but the mayor vetoed it.

The work of Kids STOP inspired a New York state official to take the legislation to the state level, and eventually the governor signed it. The legislation affected CFCs in building air conditioners as well. Major corporations, such as DuPont, responded to the law and began phasing out CFCs.

Since its founding, Kids STOP has worked with Senator Al Gore from Tennessee to write a ban on CFCs into the 1991 Clean Air Act. Kids STOP also lobbied the United Nations to provide money to Third World nations to help them in phasing out CFCs as part of the Montreal Protocol. The work of Kids STOP won recognition in 1990, receiving the President's Environmental Youth Award.

Today there are chapters of Kids STOP in every state. Kids STOP provides young people with a means to help clean up the planet. As Russell Essary demonstrated, one is never too young to make a difference in the environment. Around the world, people of all ages are banding together to fight for a cleaner, safer planet. Pollution still exists, and it knows no political boundaries. But because of the lethargy and bureaucracy of government, citizens around the world have trumpeted the environmental cause in an attempt to make the world a safer, more habitable place.

APPENDIX: FOR MORE INFORMATION

African Wildlife Foundation
1717 Massachusetts Avenue NW
Washington, DC 20036
(202) 265-8393

Citizens' Clearinghouse for
  Hazardous Waste
P.O. Box 6806
Falls Church, VA 22040
(703) 237-2249

Earth First!
P.O. Box 5871
Tucson, AZ 85703

Earth Island Institute
300 Broadway, Suite 28
San Francisco, CA 94133-3312
(415) 788-3666

Environmental Action
6930 Carroll Avenue, Suite 600
Tacoma Park, MD 20912

Environmental Defense Fund
257 Park Avenue South
New York, NY 10010
(212) 505-2100

Friends of the Earth
218 D Street SE
Washington, DC 20003
(202) 544-2600

Greenpeace USA
1436 U Street NW
Washington, DC 20009
(202) 462-1177

The Izaak Walton League of
  America
1401 Wilson Boulevard, Level B
Arlington, VA 22209
(703) 528-1818

Kids STOP (Kids Save the Planet!)
P.O. Box 471
Forest Hills, NY 11375
(718) 997-7387

National Audubon Society
700 Broadway
New York, NY 10003
(212) 979-3000

National Coalition Against
  the Misuse of Pesticides
  (NCAMP)
530 Seventh Street SE
Washington, DC 20003
(202) 543-5450

National Toxics Campaign
1168 Commonwealth Avenue
Boston, MA 02134
(617) 232-0327

National Wildlife Federation
1400 Sixteenth Street NW
Washington, DC 20036-2266
(202) 797-6800

Natural Resources Defense
  Council
40 West Twentieth Street
New York, NY 10011
(212) 727-2700

The Nature Conservancy
1815 North Lynn Street
Arlington, VA 22209
(703) 841-5300

Rainforest Action Network
301 Broadway, Suite A
San Francisco, CA 94133
(415) 398-4404

Sea Shepherd Conservation
  Society
P.O. Box 7000-S
Redondo Beach, CA 90277
(213) 373-6979

Sierra Club
P.O. Box 7959
San Francisco, CA 94120-9943
(415) 776-2211

Student Environmental Action
  Coalition (SEAC)
P.O. Box 1168
Chapel Hill, NC 27514-1168
(919) 967-4600

Union of Concerned Scientists
26 Church Street
Cambridge, MA 02238
(617) 547-5552

United States Public Interest
  Research Group (U.S. PIRG)
215 Pennsylvania Avenue SE
Washington, DC 20003
(202) 547-9707

The Wilderness Society
900 Seventeenth Street NW
Washington, DC 20006-2596
(202) 833-2300

The Worldwatch Institute
1776 Massachusetts Avenue NW
Washington, DC 20036
(202) 452-1999

World Wildlife Fund
1250 Twenty-fourth Street NW
Washington, DC 20037
(202) 293-4800

Zero Population Growth
1400 Sixteenth Street NW, Suite
  320
Washington, DC 20036
(202) 332-2200

FURTHER READING

Borrelli, Peter, ed. *Crossroads: Environmental Priorities for the Future.*
Covelo, CA: Island Press, 1988.

Bramwell, Anna. *Ecology in the 20th Century.* New Haven, CT: Yale
University Press, 1989.

Brundtland, G. H. *Our Common Future: World Commission on
Environment and Development.* New York: Oxford University Press,
1987.

Clawson, Marion. *The Federal Lands Revisited.* Washington, DC:
Resources for the Future, 1983.

Cohen, Michael P. *The Pathless Way: John Muir and American
Wilderness.* Madison: University of Wisconsin Press, 1984.

Dunlap, Thomas. *Saving America's Wildlife.* Princeton: Princeton
University Press, 1988.

Fox, Stephen. *John Muir and His Legacy: The American Conservation
Movement.* Boston: Little, Brown, 1981.

Graham, Frank. *Man's Dominion: The Story of Conservation in America.*
New York: M. Evans, 1971.

Hartzog, George B., Jr. *Battling for the National Parks.* Mt. Kisco, NY:
Moyer Bell, 1988.

Leopold, Aldo. *A Sand County Almanac.* New York: Oxford University
Press, 1949.

Livingston, John A. *One Cosmic Instant: A Natural History of Human Arrogance.* Boston: Houghton Mifflin, 1973.

McCormick, John. *Reclaiming Paradise: The Global Environmental Movement.* Bloomington: Indiana University Press, 1989.

Meine, Curt. *Aldo Leopold: His Life and Work.* Madison: University of Wisconsin Press, 1988.

Nicholson, Max. *The New Environmental Age.* New York: Cambridge University Press, 1987.

Tanner, Thomas, ed. *Aldo Leopold: The Man and His Legacy.* Ankeny, IA: Soil Conservation Society of America, 1987.

PICTURE CREDITS

GLOSSARY

carcinogenic   Cancer causing.

civil disobedience   Refusal to obey the law, usually nonviolently and often collectively, in order to force the government to make concessions or simply as a protest.

conservation   Planned management of a natural resource to prevent exploitation, destruction, or neglect.

ecotage   Sabotage used to prevent environmentally destructive practices or to garner publicity for environmental causes.

ecoteurs   Those who engage in ecotage.

global warming   The buildup of greenhouse gases in the atmosphere that is causing an increase in the temperature of the earth's climate.

grass-roots organizations   Organizations founded and governed at a local level.

greenhouse effect   The increase in the temperature of the earth's climate caused by the buildup of infrared radiation in the earth's atmosphere.

ornithologist   A zoologist who specializes in the study of birds.

ozone layer   An invisible layer of gas that shields the earth's surface by filtering out harmful ultraviolet radiation from the sun.

paleontologist   A scientist who studies the past through fossil remains.

transcendentalist movement   A philosophical movement in America, whose members generally believed in an organic universe suffused by an immanent God, the divinity of humankind, and the importance of the individual.

INDEX

founds Wilderness Society,
41
"Lifeguard of Nature" (Druzhini),
99
Love Canal, 87, 88, 89
Love Canal Home Owners
Association (LCHA), 88, 90

Manhattan Project, 78
founds *Bulletin of Atomic
Scientists,* 78
Marshall, Robert, 41, 42
Massachusetts Institute of
Technology (MIT), 76, 81,
82
Metallurgy Laboratory of the
Manhattan Project, 76
Mianus River Gorge, New York,
46
MIT. *See* Massachusetts Institute of
Technology (MIT)
Monkey Wrench Gang, The
(Abbey), 65
Monkey wrenching, 69, 71
Montreal Protocol, the, 101
Muir, John, 28–32, 35, 41, 42, 52,
69
elected president of the Sierra
Club, 29
and the Hetch Hetchy Valley
debate, 32
Mururoa Atoll, 67
My First Summer in the Sierra
(Muir), 52

Nader, Ralph, 21, 60, 61
National Committee for a Sane
Nuclear Policy (SANE), 76,
80–81
National Forest System, 40, 41

National Parks, 26, 29, 30, 31, 53,
54
National Resources Defense
Council, 49
National Toxics Campaign, 23, 90
National Wildlife, 46
National Wildlife Federation, 21,
40, 43, 44, 46
Natural Resources Defense
Council, 21
"Nature" (Emerson), 30
Nature Conservancy, 40
Nelson, Gaylord, 56
New York Sportsmen's Club, 27
New York State's Audubon
Plumage Law, 34
1918 Migratory Bird Treaty Act, 34
Nobel, Alfred, 79
Nuclear energy, 75, 76, 78
Nuclear power plants, 49, 76, 82,
83
Nuclear Regulatory Commission
(NRC), 83
Nuclear war, 75, 76, 78
Nuclear weapons, 66, 84

Ocean dumping, 23
Oceanic Society, 98
Ozone layer, 100

People Against Hazardous Landfill
Sites (PAHLs), 19, 91, 93
Pesticides, 47, 59
Phyllis Cormack, 66
Pickett, Clarence, 81
Pinchot, Gifford, 25, 31, 32, 41
Provisional Committee to Stop
Nuclear Tests, 80. *See also*
National Committee for a Sane
Nuclear Policy

(From U.S./English system units to metric system units)

Length

1 inch = 2.54 centimeters
1 foot = 0.305 meters
1 yard = 0.91 meters
1 statute mile = 1.6 kilometers (km.)

Area

1 square yard = 0.84 square meters
1 acre = 0.405 hectares
1 square mile = 2.59 square km.

Liquid Measure

1 fluid ounce = 0.03 liters
1 pint (U.S.) = 0.47 liters
1 quart (U.S.) = 0.95 liters
1 gallon (U.S.) = 3.78 liters

Weight and Mass

1 ounce = 28.35 grams
1 pound = 0.45 kilograms
1 ton = 0.91 metric tons

Temperature

1 degree Fahrenheit = 0.56 degrees Celsius or centigrade, but to convert from actual Fahrenheit scale measurements to Celsius, subtract 32 from the Fahrenheit reading, multiply the result by 5, and then divide by 9. For example, to convert 212° F to Celsius:

$$212 - 32 = 180 \times 5 = 900 \div 9 = 100° \text{ C}$$

ABOUT THE AUTHOR

ROBBIN LEE ZEFF is a freelance writer, presently living in Washington, D.C. She has a B.A. from the University of California at Berkeley and an M.A. and Ph.D. from Indiana University.

ABOUT THE EDITOR

RUSSELL E. TRAIN, currently chairman of the board of directors of the World Wildlife Fund and The Conservation Foundation, has had a long and distinguished career of government service under three presidents. In 1957 President Eisenhower appointed him a judge of the United States Tax Court. He served Lyndon Johnson on the National Water Commission. Under Richard Nixon he became under secretary of the Interior and, in 1970, first chairman of the Council on Environmental Quality. From 1973 to 1977 he served as administrator of the Environmental Protection Agency. Train is also a trustee or director of the African Wildlife Foundation; the Alliance to Save Energy; the American Conservation Association; Citizens for Ocean Law; Clean Sites, Inc.; the Elizabeth Haub Foundation; the King Mahendra Trust for Nature Conservation (Nepal); Resources for the Future; the Rockefeller Brothers Fund; the Scientists' Institute for Public Information; the World Resources Institute; and Union Carbide and Applied Energy Services, Inc. Train is a graduate of Princeton and Columbia Universities, a veteran of World War II, and currently resides in the District of Columbia.